Dedicated To Music

The Legacy of African American Church Musicians and

Music Teachers in Southern New Jersey, 1915-1990

by

Henrietta Fuller Robinson and Carolyn Cordelia Williams

with an introduction by Clement Alexander Price

Africana Homestead Legacy Publishers
Cherry Hill, New Jersey

Africana Homestead Legacy Publishers
PO Box 2957
Cherry Hill, New Jersey 08034-0265
©1997 Henrietta Fuller Robinson and Carolyn Cordelia Williams.
ALL RIGHTS RESERVED. Published 30 July 1997.
Printed on permanent/durable acid-free paper and bound in the United
States of America.
03 02 01 00 99 98 97   5 4 3 2 1

Cover design by Brian Lancaster of Omega Group III
Text design by Brian Lancaster and Carolyn Cordelia Williams

Library of Congress Cataloging-in-Publication Data

Robinson, Henrietta Fuller, 1904-
    Dedicated to music : the legacy of African American church
  musicians and music teachers in Southern New Jersey, 1915-1990 / by
  Henrietta Fuller Robinson and Carolyn Cordelia Williams ; with an
  introduction by Clement Alexander Price.
        p.   cm.
  Includes bibliographical references (p.   ) and index.
  ISBN 0-9653308-4-2 (alk. paper)
    1. Afro-American church musicians—New Jersey—Biography. 2.
  Afro-American music teachers—New Jersey—Biography. I. Williams,
  Carolyn Cordelia, 1958-   . II. Title.
  ML385.R69 1997
  780'.92'39607307499--dc21
  [B]   97-10285
                                                       CIP

Front cover photo: Senior Choir, Kaighn Avenue Baptist Church, Camden, New
Jersey, 1996. Photograph by Ron Jackson.
Back cover photo: Boys Band, New Jersey Manual Training and Industrial School
for Colored Youth, Bordentown, New Jersey, 1939. Reprint from the New Jersey
State Archives, Department of State, Trenton, New Jersey.

ABOUT THE AUTHORS

A Philadelphia native and long time resident of southern New Jersey, Henrietta Fuller Robinson is noted for her remarkable sixty year career as a music teacher, pianist, organist, choir director, vocalist, and talent promoter. Formerly an elementary school teacher in the New Jersey public schools, she has self-published *Stories of New Jersey*, a coloring book for children, *My Jerseyland*, a brief illustrated history of New Jersey, and a song lyric, *My Jerseyland, A Prayer For Our State*. *Dedicated to Music* is the crowning glory of her lifetime achievements.

Since leaving a memorable career in research and clinical science, Carolyn Cordelia Williams has worked as a freelance writer, historical researcher, lecturer, project director, and non-profit organization manager. A native of Cherry Hill, New Jersey, she is the co-author of scientific papers, and the author of feature articles on African American and African Canadian history. Williams's auspicious entry into publishing commenced with her founding of Africana Homestead Legacy Publishers and the issuance of this title. Also a student of music, her artistic credits include performances as a violoncellist and vocalist.

CONTENTS

DEDICATION AND ACKNOWLEDGMENTS

To my mother and father, Henrietta Jane (Booth) Fuller, who taught me to love music with greater inspiration, and Hercules A.Fuller; to my late husband, Blanchard W. Robinson, Sr., my three children, Alonzo, Blanchard Jr., and Henrietta, my seven brothers and sisters, fellow musicians, and my students; also to my fellow choir members, and the Sunday School music director, Professor Francis A. Clark, at Allen AME Church, Philadelphia, Pennsylvania; to Marian Anderson, my voice teacher, who encouraged me to train youth to sing spiritual praise to God, and Anna W. Cheston, my music teacher at the Philadelphia Normal School.

Henrietta Fuller Robinson

To my father and mother, Joseph Sherman (deceased) and Catherine Veturia (Archer) Williams, Sr., my family, and friends; to the musicians and music teachers in my family whose accomplishments are the source of my inspiration: Carl Rossini Diton; Samuel and Phoebe (Harvey) Diton; J. Harvey Hebron; Josephine Harvey; Emma Harvey; Charlotte Harvey; my parents; Elizabeth (Riley) McFadden; Ada Seth Shaw; Charles Williams Sr.; Roland Wiggins, Ph.D.; Marie Valentine. Their stories will soon follow.

Carolyn C. Williams

We gratefully acknowledge:

The New Jersey Historical Commission (NJHC), Department of State, Trenton, New Jersey, for funding the publication of *Dedicated to Music*.
Giles R. Wright, Director of the Afro-American History Program of the NJHC, for his firm belief that this project merited its support, for proposing our collaboration and facilitating our meeting, and his invaluable technical assistance.
Mary R. Murrin, Director of the Grant-In-Aid Program of the NJHC, for her important technical assistance.
Clement Alexander Price, for his splendid, perceptive essay and useful advice.
Brian Lancaster, for his exceptional designs and artistic direction.
Ella Forbes, for her timely and astute review comments.
The informants, including musicians, relatives, students, choir members, and associates, who extended gracious hospitality, gave forthright, thoughtful interviews, and willingly shared treasured photographs and memorabilia.

PREFACE

Henrietta Fuller Robinson and I met in late November of 1993, introduced by Giles R. Wright II, Director of the Afro-American History Program of the New Jersey Historical Commission (NJHC), who proposed that we collaborate on a study of black church musicians and music teachers in southern New Jersey, and publish the result as a book. His reasons were manifold. Greatly admiring Henrietta's marvelous career in music, and having read her manuscript, *The Forgotten Music Teacher*, he was intent on helping her realize her dream of publishing profiles of her life, and her peers's lives. Moreover, from his knowledge of my work-in-progress on musician Carl Rossini Diton, research of other nineteenth and twentieth century African American musicians in New Jersey and Pennsylvania, and musical background, Giles knew I was a good candidate to serve as her co-author. He also thought it critical to document this engaging aspect of our state's history.

Recognizing the merits of a joint effort, Henrietta and I gladly proceeded. By submitting proposals to the NJHC, I obtained funding for research, manuscript preparation, publication costs, and to hire two consultants: historian Clement A. Price, to write the book's introduction; graphic designer Brian Lancaster, to create its cover design and advise on text layout.

Our work started May 1994. Although separated in age by several generations, we had an easy rapport. Conducting an oral interview to complete her narrative, I first recorded ten hours of Henrietta's memories. At each visit, she shared with me her large collection of photographs and memorabilia, an invaluable documentation of her life, her associates, and key local organizations. Occasionally interrupting a student's lessons, I also witnessed her obvious joy in teaching music, and her pupils's great admiration of her.

Then, traveling much of southern New Jersey in spring and summer of 1995, I interviewed several musicians and music teachers, their family members and friends. My informants's enthusiasm and hospitality was exceptional. Meanwhile, searching regional archives, libraries, and Henrietta's collection yielded added highlights for the biographical dictionary's profiles.

Needless to say, Henrietta and I are very proud of *Dedicated to Music: The Legacy of African American Church Musicians and Music Teachers in Southern New Jersey, 1915-1990*. It is the crowning glory to her long, and amazing life. For me, this work has dually fostered my growth as a historiographer and a publisher. Preserving the legacy of so many talented and devoted individuals, for both of us, has been deeply satisfying, a true labor of love.

Carolyn Cordelia Williams, 1997

INTRODUCTION

Composing The Community

Blacks Making and Teaching Music in Southern New Jersey

In 1957, at the age of fifty-nine, a far distance from his early childhood and years after he became one of the twentieth-century's most
famous American singers, Paul Robeson remembered the importance of
music to his young life in Princeton, New Jersey. Within the town's old
Negro community, "this hemmed-in world," as Robeson called it, "where
home must be theater and concert hall and social center, there was a
warmth of song. Songs of love and longing, songs of trials and triumphs,
deep-flowing rivers and rollicking brooks, hymn-song and ragtime ballad, gospel and blues and the healing comfort to be found in the illimit-
able sorrow of the spirituals." [1]

Robeson's sentimental remembrance is echoed when Afro-Americans speak or write recollections of life within their communities. Music,
that most tenacious of the race's cultural properties to survive the slavery
period, is also among the best remembered. No other artifact approaches
its omnipresence, its ability to take one inside of the expressiveness of the
Afro-American experience. Whether belted out by blues or gospel singers or sung with nuanced restraint by formally trained concert performers; whether played in the vernacular on time-worn instruments, or presented in highly polished compositions, music is a connecting tissue in
black community life. It has helped twentieth-century blacks understand
the travail and hopes of their forbears, mindful of life under slavery and
a momentous event in black folklife—the news of Emancipation. When
freedom came for southern blacks, music sustained far into the future
the emotional context of life during America's ignoble past. The songs
composed by those whom James Weldon Johnson called the black and
unknown bards of the South's plantations, and their progeny, became
powerful symbols of black cultural distinctiveness and, perhaps, the stur-
diest common ground for creative expression. "Black Americans," Toni
Morrison has observed, "were sustained and healed and nurtured by the
translation of their experience into art above all in the music." [2]

We have known for the longest time that the musical arts found a
home in the Negro church, the most revered of race institutions. Churches
figured prominently in the rise of music as a vehicle for creativity and
commentary on Afro-American emotions. As veritable centers of community life, their influence was ubiquitous when and wherever blacks
sang, played or composed music. Churches enabled their parishioners to

create, mentor and perform. They also fostered an appreciation of the culture of Afro-America, and· at a time when modernism encouraged curiosity across the racial bar, these same bodies introduced blacks to the music of other cultures and societies.

Yet, we know little of the church musicians and music teachers whose expertise and stature within their communities made this all possible. Despite a disproportionately large representation within the black professional class, local musicians have remained largely anonymous historical actors, rarely receiving the attention customarily given to local ministers, physicians, business leaders, social workers and other professionals.[3]

This indifference is regrettable, as musicians played a substantial role in promoting cultural norms and social interaction during the segregation era and contemporary times. Those who are interested in examining the ways in which twentieth-century blacks gave meaning to their lives and those troubled by the stunning decline of black communities since the late 1960's will have to examine the accomplishments, and the memories, of the individuals who sustained interest in music coming from the community.

My memory of what it once meant to be a member of a black community during the Jim Crow era can be traced to the early influence of church musicians at my home church, Israel Colored (later Christian) Methodist Episcopal Church in Washington, D.C. There, during the 1950's and early 1960's, I became aware that Sarah Moxley, Serena Taylor, and Althea Bunton, indefatigable and graceful women who played the church piano and organ and led the congregation in song, kept alive important cultural traditions bequeathed by my distant forebears. During my childhood, these church musicians, whom I remember loomed large every Sunday morning and at funerals and other special occasions, enabled me and my generation of Civil Rights Movement children to link their wide range of feelings to music.[4]

For many blacks coming of age at the twilight of the segregation era, church musicians and music teachers arouse indelible memories. Sarah Moxley, Serena Taylor, and Althea Bunton, who were instrumental in my upbringing, and hundreds of their counterparts in churches throughout the nation, were formidable figures in large part because of the centrality of their roles as musicians. They nurtured black children through preparation for first public performances as budding musicians. They formed and led choral ensembles which, as symbols of discipline, respectability, and musicianship, promoted civic life and a wholesome framework for black entertainment. Their musicianship provided a powerful emotional context for church services, especially on those occasions when memory and music intersected at a favorite hymn or spiritual. As emblems of decorum and respectability, their lives challenged the contradictions and perceived disparities existing between Afro-American and Euro-American culture. And in recent years, as old black communities have become far more isolated and impoverished places, those who played and taught music remind many of a time when life there was more secure. Our memories of what these individuals meant to our upbringing and values helps to define black community life and identity.[5]

Students of Afro-American history rely a great deal upon the individual and collective memories of veterans of the past. What can be remembered and documented by seemingly ordinary blacks is indispensable to the way history is now understood and written. Personal memories of the past can partially compensate for the poorly-documented episodes of black community life and the traditional bias against the important roles played by women, workers, and migrants. And, too, memory is virtually essential to an understanding of the largely obscured history of local, community-based organizations, many of which existed with too little attention given to the preservation of written records. In those organizations and communities, Robeson's aptly described "hemmed in worlds," memory resonates with both personal and social meaning.[6]

With the publication of *Dedicated to Music: The Legacy of African American Church Musicians and Music Teachers in Southern New Jersey, 1915-1990*, the importance of memory in documenting the history of modern black New Jersey life and culture is given center stage. This is an endearing opus from a veteran of the past, Henrietta Fuller Robinson, and co-authored by Carolyn Cordelia Williams. It is also unique and valuable to the study of community formation in the southern counties of New Jersey, where freedom for blacks dawned at the founding of the Republic and where the profound advantages and difficulties of freedom were first observed.[7] Not since the Camden County Historical Society's

1984 publication, *The Black Experience in Southern New Jersey,* have the internal dynamics of black communities in southern New Jersey received such attention, nor is there a more carefully detailed portrait of individuals in those places. *Dedicated to Music* enhances our understanding of twentieth-century southern New Jersey, where blacks had considerable control over their daily lives as a result of community institutions, cultural awareness and the dedication of scores of women and men to racial uplift.

Scholars of southern New Jersey's black past have argued that by the late nineteenth century, black residents there had created cohesive communities, which were at once emblematic of progress and a desire for shelter from racial discrimination. Through an array of sacred and secular organizations that conferred a sense of privacy and autonomy, blacks attended to their own interests and survived the unsavory effects of racial intolerance. Southern New Jersey's tradition of segregation in public life was reinforced by a preference by blacks for social and cultural separatism. Early black residents of southern New Jersey had established towns of their own long before the rise of Booker T. Washington and his famous credo of black achievement through autonomy. They advocated group self development in education, in contrast to black opinion in other parts of New Jersey. For nearly half of the twentieth century, as black leaders in the northern counties of the State railed against segregation in public schools, their counterparts in southern counties held that official segregation was not necessarily inimical to black progress. The historian Giles R. Wright has observed that some blacks in the southern part of the State tacitly accepted segregated black schools "because they provided a measure of autonomy and self-determination," provided professional opportunities unknown to blacks in supposedly integrated districts, and "spared black pupils the racial indignities often encountered in integrated classrooms."[8]

The Negro church personified the inherent advantages of blacks controlling the most important institutions in their communities. During much of the twentieth century, southern New Jersey's black churches in Camden, Burlington, Moorestown, Mount Laurel, Lawnside, and Pennington, among others, spawned a diverse network of individuals, organizations and interests that responded to the needs of their communities. Musicians and music teachers were important figures in that emerging configuration of professionals and working-class laborers who were dependent upon the support of fellow blacks. Their efforts to popularize music, to keep it at the center of the worship service, and to expand training in instrumental music and singing made black residents remarkably literate in musical culture. And as a result of their church affiliations, their contacts and collaborations with fellow musicians throughout the greater southern New Jersey and Philadelphia region, and the outpouring of musical programs within and beyond the church, the individuals featured in *Dedicated to Music* acquired a social prominence and status in the State that was denied them in other pursuits.

The sacred music that church musicians performed was, of course, a fixture throughout Afro-America; it was a motif for social and cultural change. Folk spirituals, folk gospels and gospel hymns, though created out of the slavery and immediate post-slavery periods, survived and sustained memories of the past well into the twentieth century. After the Great Migration brought thousands of blacks from southern states to the North, few churches could succeed in attracting new parishioners, nor could they hold onto old ones, without acknowledging in the worship service music sung and performed in the South and the Christian migrant's memories of a painful past. Musicians, in this sense, were trustees of what Lenola Allen Sommerville calls "the yeast that has given shape and content to the African American religious experience." And as one church musician has noted, they provided "a doorway into worship." They were at the vortex of modern black cultural expression at a time when a significant number of blacks were church goers.[9]

And so church musicians contributed to what might be called the democratization of twentieth-century black religious culture. Many were conversant with, and encouraged as teachers an appreciation of, a wide range of musical genres, including the sacred and secular, the classical and the popular. In this sense, they were instrumental in connecting, or cross fertilizing, varied musical genres at a time when black communities were both expanding and becoming increasingly demarcated along class lines. The music of a particular church often reflected these changes— the interplay and tension between parishioners of different social standing, between the so-called Old Settlers of a particular community and recent migrants from the South or other areas. Within that diverse arena of worship, social contact and cultural exchange, where music was both the mettle of the service and a reflection of a range of social and cultural values, an intraracial discourse between classes and men and women was articulated.[10] It would seem that over the course of the first half of the twentieth century, formally trained church musicians introduced more stylized European and Afro-American compositions into the repertoire of black choral groups. Because musicians in some churches were given the authority to decide on the music to be performed, they played a major role in helping black communities negotiate a modern culture across the lines of class, status and regional culture.[11]

In acknowledging the role of social class and status in determining musical taste, we must also take into account the extraordinary presence of women in the making and teaching of music in southern New Jersey's black communities. Indeed, during much of the century black women in the State were musicians in proportionately greater numbers than was the case for white women and black women nationally. Of the thirty-three musicians' lives chronicled here, including Henrietta Fuller Robinson's, twenty-two are women. Students of Afro-American and women's history will not be surprised at the relatively large representation of black women in the ranks of professional musicians and music teachers. Just as black women were actively engaged in advocating social reform and protest, so too were they active in promoting cultural life, especially during the early twentieth century when professional opportunities for women were limited. Musical training and the professional opportunities it fostered enabled women to secure important places in the community as pianists, organists, conductors, and musical mentors. As a result, they helped to institutionalize choral singing and the playing of instruments, and they seemed to have had enormous influence in reconciling changing musical tastes with traditional church liturgy. To have accomplished this in a male-dominated church hierarchy was nothing short of remarkable, and compels a further reconsideration of gender relations and the role of women in the development of black communities throughout New Jersey.

Aside from what Robinson's and Williams's study reveals about the energy, talent and organizational acumen of women in promoting music in southern New Jersey black communities, we are encouraged to consider their influence in cultivating civic culture in black neighborhoods. They, after all, made the two most important dwellings of their lives, their homes and their churches, havens for music. There black women fostered civility, community appreciation for social respectability, and decorum. These were duties long associated with the perceived role of middle-class women in the larger society, but they carried a far more empowering meaning for women in black society. As historian Elsa Barkley Brown has observed, black women used their church roles "to direct the men in their communities and the affairs of those communities." Having limited access to male dominated professions such as the clergy, law and medicine, women located their interests and their talents within the expansive network of music making and teaching. That role, which Henrietta Fuller Robinson's career brilliantly demonstrates, gave women considerable influence over the ways in which black communities evolved during the century and positioned themselves for the future.[12]

Students of Afro-American history increasingly examine modern black life from such vantage points as local community organizations and leaders, the affirming experience of women, the customs of workers and the poor, protest activities before the Civil Rights Movement, and the tenacity of folk culture and memory into the twentieth century. The advent of this so-called "new black history" has shed light on dynamic features of a largely obscured past, especially the way in which blacks, facing considerable odds against progress and community integrity, gave agency and meaning to their vulnerable lives.[13] *Dedicated to Music* informs this new interest in the internal qualities of black life; it introduces us to the small details of the past where remembrance of tradition and ceremony, a sense of place, and cultural identity converge to make communities out of the areas where most blacks lived, largely unappreciated and undesired as neighbors except by their own. With this remarkable book, New Jersey's Afro-American history becomes far more accessible and the achievements of a uniquely talented group of twentieth-century race men and women is, finally, a matter of historical record.

Clement Alexander Price
Newark, New Jersey

NOTES AND REFERENCES

1. Paul Robeson, *Here I Stand* (Boston: Beacon Press, 1958), p. 15.

2. Eileen Southern, *The Music of Black Americans, A History* (New York: W.W. Norton & Company, 1971); Lawrence W. Levine, *Black Culture and Black Consciousness: Afro-American Folk Thought From Slavery To Freedom* (New York: Oxford University Press, pp. 5–19, pp. 190–297. On the centrality of black music in the modern African diaspora, see Paul Gilroy, "Sounds Authentic: Black Music, Ethnicity, and the Challenge of a Changing Same," *Black Music Research Journal* XI (Fall 1991); An overview of scholarship on black music can be found in Doris Evans McGinty, "Black Scholars on Black Music: The Past, The Present, and the Future," *Black Music Research Journal* XIII (Spring 1993); Morrison's observation, given in an interview, is considerably expanded upon in Paul Gilroy, *The Black Atlantic: Modernity and Double Consciousness* (Cambridge: Harvard University Press, 1993), p. 78.

3. A useful volume on black American music teachers is Lemuel Berry, Jr., *Biographical Dictionary of Black Musicians and Music Educators* (Guthrie, Oklahoma: Midwest Publishing Company, 1978). I thank Trish Morris Yamba for bringing this publication to my attention.

4. Interview with Anna Christine Price, my mother, and Jarmila Louise Price, my sister, on May 28, 1996. My home church, Israel C.M.E. Church, addressed the challenges imposed by the diversity of its congregation in pragmatic ways: it sought to satisfy a broad range of musical tastes through choral presentations that ranged from Negro vernacular music to highbrow European classics. Hence, there was the Senior Choir, comprised of the "better" voices in the Church, which performed demanding choral works requiring the talents of a director and the Gospel Choir, which presented, usually without direction, spirited renditions of traditional Spirituals and gospel compositions.

5. Earl Lewis, "Connecting Memory, Self, and the Power of Place in African American Urban History," *Journal of Urban History* 21 (March 1995), 351–367.

6. David Thelen, "Memory and American History," *Journal of Urban History*, 75 (March 1989) 1117-1129.

7. Clement Alexander Price, "The Cause in Which We are Mutually Engaged: Quakers and the Dawn of Black Freedom in New Jersey," in M.M. Pernot, ed. *After Freedom* (Burlington, NJ: Burlington County Historical Society, 1987), pp. ii–viii.

8. Spencer R. Crew, "Making Their Own Way: Black Social and Institutional Life in Camden, New Jersey, 1860–1920," in *The Black Experience in Southern New Jersey: Papers Presented at a Symposium, February 11 & 12, 1984* (Camden: Camden County Historical Society, 1984), pp. 19–29; Clement Alexander Price, "We Knew Our Place, We Knew Our Way: Lessons From the Black Past of Southern New Jersey," in Bruce Ransom, ed., *Blacks in New Jersey, 1986 Report* (Newark, NJ: Seventh Annual Report of the New Jersey Public Policy and Research Institute. 1986), pp. 10–23; Giles R. Wright, *Afro-Americans in New Jersey: A Short History* (Trenton, NJ: New Jersey Historical Commission, 1988), p. 52. Also, for an oral-history based study of southern New Jersey education for blacks see Wynetta Devore, "The Education of Blacks in New Jersey, 1900–1930," Ed.D. diss, Rutgers University, 1980. The most recently published study of Afro-American history in New Jersey, which includes many interesting observations on black life in the southern counties, is L.A. Greene, "A History of Afro-Americans in New Jersey," *The Journal of the Rutgers University Libraries* (LVI). For a thoughtful perspective on contemporary historical scholarship on the strategies by which post-Emancipation blacks coped with the realities of racial exclusion and injustice in the late nineteenth century, see: Earl Lewis, *In Their Own Interests: Race, Class, and Power in twentieth Century Norfolk, Virginia* (Berkeley: University of California Press, 1991), pp. 8–28.

9. Lenola Allen-Sommerville, "African American 'Church Music' in the Classroom: A Cultural Portrait," *Religion and Public Education* 20 (1993) p. 77; interview with Judy Doll, Newark, New Jersey, May 19, 1996.

10. Earl Lewis, "Connecting Memory, Self, and the Power of Place in African American History," p. 358.

11. This is not to suggest that church musicians could not select music without considerable direction from ministers. Many did not. In recent years, some Protestant congregations have elevated the status of church musicians by designating them as ministers of music, which one might assume, places them on a much higher plane of authority within their churches.
12. Elsa Barkley Brown, "Constructing a Lie and a Community: A Story of the Life of the Life of Maggie Lena Walker," *OAH Magazine of History* 7 (Summer 1993), 28.
13. Thomas C. Holt, "Whither Now and Why," in Darlene Clark Hine, ed., The State of Afro-American History (Baton Rouge, Louisiana State University Press, 1986), pp. 1–10.

PART ONE

Henrietta Fuller Robinson

A Life Dedicated to Music

Inspired by her great love for music, Henrietta Fuller Robinson has engaged in this art form in a variety of ways for virtually ninety-three years of her life. In southern New Jersey she spent almost sixty years fashioning an extraordinary professional music career, functioning as a music teacher, pianist, organist, choir director, and talent promoter. Remarkably, she was also the very last active music teacher from her generation of multi-talented, classically trained black church musicians who served the black community of southern New Jersey for the better part of the 20th century.

Four very distinct periods comprise Henrietta's full and productive life. The first can be called her "early years." Covering the first twenty years of her life, this period ends as she completes her formal education at a normal school. The second period of her life stretches from 1925 to 1937 and encompasses most of her professional training as a classical musician. During this period she also works as a school teacher and becomes a wife and a mother. In 1937, Henrietta moved from her native Philadelphia to southern New Jersey and began her long years serving as a church musician and music teacher in this area. Equally important, she emerged as a leader in her field and ultimately served as president of the Camden Chapter of the National Association of Negro Musicians. Henrietta stepping down as president of the chapter in 1986 marks the close of this period. Her final years, best called her semi-retirement since she has remained active in the music world to a certain extent, constitute the fourth period of her life, one lasting into the mid 1990's.

Henrietta was born at 2127 Catharine Street in Philadelphia, Pennsylvania, on April 14, 1904, to Hercules Alexander Fuller and Jane (Booth) Fuller. The Fuller children, four boys and four girls, were born and raised in Philadelphia: in order by age, they were William Henry, Albert Edward, Grace, Annabelle, Hercules Alexander Jr., Henrietta Booth, Ethel Marie, and Raymond Joyce.

Born in Norfolk, Virginia in 1864, Henrietta's father was a lively and alert person. His mother had died when he was two years old, so his grandmother raised him. At the age of fourteen, having had little education, he left home to work on a boat in Norfolk's harbor. For two years he traveled back and forth between the cities of Baltimore and Norfolk. This, his first job, earned him the family nick-name of "sailor." Eventually, Henrietta's father decided to stay in Baltimore, where he had made new friends. After obtaining work as a stable boy, he became friends with William Henry Booth, who worked in the stables with him. Having no relatives in Baltimore, he visited the Booth family home quite often. There he became acquainted with William's sister, whom he later married.

Henrietta's mother and namesake was born in 1870 in Baltimore, Maryland. In childhood she received some education and completed grammar school. Besides having a keen interest in education, the Booth family was devoutly religious and her mother's father served as the choir leader at their church. This role was one reason that he had an organ in the home while Henrietta's mother was growing up. Its presence in the home led to her, as a teenager, taking organ lessons from a teacher who came to their house. As entertainment, Henrietta's mother especially enjoyed playing hymns. Sometime after she turned eighteen, her mother, who also took a course in dressmaking, moved to Philadelphia and earned money doing housework, employment in which she did very well for several years.

Two or so years after her mother left Baltimore, Henrietta's father came to Philadelphia; he looked for work and he visited Henrietta's mother. Their friendship grew, and in 1893 her parents married in a ceremony in Atlantic City, New Jersey. The young couple settled in South Philadelphia. By then, her father had a job working as coachman for Dr. W. W. Keene, a chief surgeon at Jefferson Medical College in Philadelphia. Her mother stayed home, caring for the family, since she did not believe married women should work outside of the household. Throughout their life, both of Henrietta's parents worked very hard to provide for their large family; they passed this important work ethic along to their children.

As was customary at the time, her parents stayed with someone when they were first married. Later on they rented a small house in South Philadelphia where they lived for three or four years. Sometime later they moved to a house in the same neighborhood, at 2127 Catharine Street. This is where Henrietta was born. Then the family moved again, living in several houses in the area along Seventeenth Street. Finally they moved to a house on Bainbridge Street near Seventeenth.

On Bainbridge Street their home was a small, ordinary house with two floors and a big back yard, that her mother liked because she said it enabled the children to play outside. The neighborhood was mixed, having whites who were from the South, quite a number of Irish residents, and some Italians. It did not have many black families.

The Fuller children, including Henrietta, attended the Chester A. Arthur School at Twentieth and Catharine Streets. Following primary school they attended grammar school, the Edwin M. Stanton School, located at Seventeenth and Christian Streets. They did not start school until they were six years old because her mother, fearing they would get lost, insisted that they know how to write their name

Above left: Hercules Alexander Fuller, a native of Norfolk, Virginia, was a sailor in his youth, then worked as a coachman for a surgeon in Philadelphia.

Below, left: An expert dressmaker, Henrietta Jane Booth was born in Baltimore, Maryland. Pictured here in one of her creations, she moved to Philadelphia as a young woman.

Photos, circa late 1880's, collection of Henrietta Fuller Robinson.

Left: Sitting on their front stoop, Henrietta and her siblings were photographed by an itinerant photographer in Philadelphia, the summer of 1907.

Below: All eight Fuller children in the 1930's. (Two separate poses, combined by digital imaging.) Photos collection of Henrietta Fuller Robinson.

Standing, left to right: William Henry, Albert Edward, Hercules Alexander Jr., Raymond Joyce, Ethel Marie, Henrietta Booth. Seated, l. to r.: Annabelle, Grace.

and address before attending school. Thus taught by her mother and older brothers and sisters, Henrietta learned to write her name and address at a relatively early age.

By the time she entered school, Henrietta had developed a strong interest in music. Her mother's keen interest in music especially influenced Henrietta. The family had an organ, the type you pumped with your feet, and her mother played on it some familiar hymns, such as *Just as I Am, Jesus is Calling For Thee*, and *Blessed Assurance*. This meant that Henrietta and her siblings were exposed to religious music from birth.

Furthermore, as the family's first music teacher, Henrietta's mother taught all of her children how to play the keyboard, and sing in harmony. Indeed, singing as a group was part of the family routine, just a part of home life.

Henrietta was nine when she first tried to play the family instrument herself. By that time the Fullers had a J. C. Heppe piano. A music teacher, Janon Maginley, a young woman whose mother was interested in music too, came to the house to give lessons. Miss Maginley worked with Henrietta's mother and oldest sister for a while. Very eager to learn, Henrietta peeped around the living room door to see and listen to the teacher. Their next teacher, a German woman, also came to the house to give lessons and Henrietta's other sister and older brother joined the family music class.

Finally, when her brothers and sisters started leaving home, Henrietta had the piano to herself. She asked her mother questions about how to play, and her mother taught her a bit more. Her mother suggested things for Henrietta to practice and listened to her while she played, always offering encouragement.

During this period, Henrietta developed two other interests that she later incorporated into her work in music. One was her interest in Negro history, developed as a result of her parents' conversations about great Negro political leaders, such as Frederick Douglass and Booker T. Washington. Aware of the need to celebrate black achievement, as an adult Henrietta would thus honor the work of black classical musicians. Sewing also interested Henrietta. Taught first by her mother, Henrietta would later expand her dressmaking skills and sew choir robes for various churches.

The Fuller family attended Allen African Methodist Episcopal (AME) Church, at Seventeenth and Bainbridge, just around the corner from where they lived. Henrietta was an avid Sunday school student who enjoyed singing the hymns of the Sunday school. An accomplished musician, Francis Alfred Clark, called Professor Clark, directed the church's music program. A composer and arranger who

7

had collaborated on several hymns with Reverend Charles Albert Tindley (1859-1933), one of the earliest creators of gospel music, Professor Clark provided Henrietta with a rich musical experience that fostered her interest in music. Singing lead in the Junior Department provided her with her first chance to sing and entertain in public.

After attending grammar school, Henrietta continued her education, unlike her older siblings who went to work. At the Philadelphia High School for Girls Henrietta's interest in music continued, and she has never forgotten the music teacher there, Helen Cheston. An older woman with white hair who had been teaching music for a long time, Cheston taught Henrietta and her classmates the theory of music, structures of chords, scales, and other things. She was also a composer of many songs and taught at the Philadelphia Normal School, which was four blocks away.

Henrietta entered the Philadelphia Normal School at Thirteenth and Spring Garden Streets, after graduating high school. The year was 1922. Many Philadelphia Girls High students attended the Philadelphia Normal School, while others attended schools such as the University of Pennsylvania, and Wellesley College.

As a student in the Normal School, originally a school exclusively for girls, Henrietta studied pedagogy, that is the art of teaching. The companion school for boys was called the School of Pedagogy. When the latter school was closed, the boys and girls both attended the Philadelphia Normal School. This occurred around the same time that Henrietta completed her studies.

When Henrietta graduated from the Normal School in the midwinter term of 1925, she was proud to have her name listed in an article and her photograph published in the February 14 edition of the *Philadelphia Tribune*, the city's well-known black newspaper. Her diploma qualified her to work as a substitute teacher in the Philadelphia public schools. To Henrietta, however, such a position was not very satisfactory, because you only worked three or four days a month. It was not satisfactory to her family either; they said they could not have anybody moping around the house all the time. So later that year, after substituting for a few months, Henrietta applied to teach full time in New Jersey and was hired for the fall term.

Henrietta's initial assignment was in a little country school in Elk Township, Gloucester County, about one or two miles from Glassboro. This school, way back in the woods, was newly built and had only two rooms. She and another woman were the schools only teachers.

While her colleague instructed the higher grades, Henrietta taught the first and second grades. There were also a few children who were not qualified for first grade; called them the beginner's class. She taught the two, or sometimes three, grade levels by giving seat work to some of her students, while working directly with the remaining children. Although she liked working in the school, she was dissatisfied with the pay, which was nine hundred dollars a year. After two years, Henrietta left for a job that paid more money.

During her two years of employment at the Elk Township school, Henrietta boarded with her fellow teacher during the week; she returned to Philadelphia on weekends, traveling by train. Working near the newly built Glassboro State College gave Henrietta the chance for further study. She enrolled in classes at the college that enabled her to receive the State Teaching Certificate for Elementary Education.

In her next job Henrietta worked at the Lawnside Public School, in Lawnside, New Jersey. Founded as Snowhill at the end of the eighteenth century, the community was an important Underground Railroad station and the State's first all-black town to incorporate (in 1926) as a municipality. Henrietta taught from fourth to eighth grade at the grammar school. Since she was closer to home and her pay was eleven hundred dollars, she liked this job considerably better. Unlike the Elk Township school where Henrietta taught all subjects, the Lawnside School assigned teachers to specific departments, such that she only taught English, Art, and Music.

Simultaneous to teaching in New Jersey, Henrietta continued her music pursuits. In 1924 at age twenty she had joined her church's senior choir. Singing in the alto section, she was often a featured soloist.

The next year, Henrietta began studying voice with Marian Anderson, the famed singer. One of her church's Sunday School teachers, Mary Dawson, who was an acquaintance of Miss Anderson, encouraged to do this. Since Henrietta's family and the Anderson family had lived around the corner from each other and had become well acquainted when was a little girl, she also knew of Marian Anderson. Consequently, Henrietta contacted Marian Anderson, who at the time was working as a music teacher and pursuing her concert career, and arranged to take lessons on Friday afternoons, after returning from teaching in New Jersey.

Henrietta's private study with Marian Anderson, who gave lessons in her home in South Philadelphia on Martin Street, near Twentieth and Fitzwater Streets, lasted for one year. She was the first to teach her diaphragmatic breathing; the great difference this made in her tonal quality shocked Henrietta. The only songs Anderson taught her to sing were Negro spirituals, including Anderson's favorite, *Deep*

River. Henrietta thought her celebrated teacher was extremely personable, unpretentious, and somewhat reticent. Admiring Marian Anderson's success, she also aspired to become a concert artist.

Because of Anderson's need to travel to Europe to further her career, Henrietta found another voice teacher, Madame Rosalia Phillipe, whose studio was at Twentieth and Spruce Streets. Of Italian extraction, she had sung with the Paris Opera Company. Phillipe introduced Henrietta to classical diction. In her lessons, lasting for one and a half years, she learned to sing arias in Italian, *Caro Mio Ben, Lasciate Mi Morire,* and a few others.

During the period Henrietta taught at the Lawnside School and studied vocal music, she met her future husband, Blanchard W. Robinson. This happened through Henrietta's participation in her church's Youth Fellowship program. As representatives of their respective churches, with Blanchard belonging to Union AME Church at Sixteenth and Fairmount, the two became officers of the City in Youth Fellowship program, organized by twelve AME churches in Philadelphia. Blanchard served as president; Henrietta was the secretary.

Blanchard was born October 26, 1903 in Marked Tree, Arkansas. Although his father was a preacher and a member of the board of education in this little country town, the family essentially earned a living by growing cotton as sharecroppers. After finishing high school, Blanchard moved to Little Rock where he attended Shorter College, an AME school. Wanting to become a dentist, he decided to come to Philadelphia to enroll in the School of Mechanical Dentistry.

Since Blanchard's plans to study dentistry did not evolve, he obtained a job as a janitor shortly after arriving in Philadelphia. His next position was as mail clerk in the U.S. Post Office. During this time he was also an active church worker, and this brought him into contact with Henrietta.

Henrietta and Blanchard were married in 1928, after a short courtship and just before the Great Depression. She was twenty-four and he was twenty-five. Their first child, Alonzo, whom they named after her husband's brother, was born a year later; their second child, Blanchard Jr., was born in 1931. During these first years of marriage, the couple lived in South Philadelphia, in four different houses.

With the onslaught of the Great Depression, earning money became difficult for the couple. The Post Office changed Blanchard's work from full time to a substitute position, inducing him to take a job working with a paperhanger. At the same time, he obtained a real estate license, then was employed by a real estate lawyer on a part-time basis. Also to augment the family's income, Henrietta started

Henrietta and Blanchard married just before the Great Depression's onset.

Photographs, circa early 1920's, collection of Henrietta Fuller Robinson.

working in a restaurant for two hours a day during lunch time, so she could still care for her children.

In 1932 the couple moved to Oakford Street and began buying their first house. By then Henrietta had obtained a job sewing, earning fifteen dollars a week. This lasted about a year, and was followed by employment with the federal government's Works Progress Administration (WPA). In the WPA Federal Music Project training program, conducted by Frances Clark, a splendid music teacher who directed the New School for Music in Princeton, New Jersey, Henrietta studied piano pedagogy at the Settlement Music School, at Fourth and Queen in South Philadelphia. Since marriage and motherhood effectively ended her aspirations towards a career as a concert singer, Henrietta considered teaching music a very suitable alternative.

Teaching in the WPA program marked the start of Henrietta's professional music career. From 1933 to 1937, earning twenty-five dollars a week, she worked in settlement houses, (e.g., St. John's Settlement House), community centers, YWCA's (e.g., The YWCA at Sixteenth and Catharine Streets), YMCA's, and social service agencies (e.g., the Bureau for Colored Children in West Philadelphia). While she regularly taught piano and voice, at some of her work sites she also taught English and Social Studies.

Sometime around 1935, Henrietta joined the Philadelphia Music Teachers Association, an inter-racial organization formed by Theodore Presser, a prominent music publisher whose store was at Seventeenth and Chestnut Streets in Philadelphia. Among its activities were monthly lectures on different aspects of music performance and education. Held in the auditorium at the John Wanamaker's store, the lectures featured well-known local and national music artists.

Natalie Hinderas, the great African-Amerian classical pianist, delivered one lecture that Henrietta has always remembered. Hinderas spoke on the work of black classical musicians, especially the work of R. Nathaniel Dett, sparking Henrietta's interest in these musicians. Moreover, Dett became one of her favorite classical musicians; Playing many of his compositions as solos in her recitals, Henrietta's favorite was *His Song,* the song of a very dejected black man who suddenly becomes inspired.

As Henrietta's work under the WPA program progressed, her husband found a full time job working with American Woodmen, a fraternal organization, selling insurance. The couple's improved financial situation, and their concern about the increase of crime in their neighborhood, prompted their decision to let the house go that they were buying in Philadelphia. They sold it and bought a farm in southern New Jersey for one hundred dollars. Having a bungalow with six acres of ground, it was located in a rural area of Evesham Township, approximately one mile from Berlin.

As the couple settled into life in the country, they cleared their land, planted vegetables, and raised chickens and pigs. Blanchard's Arkansas farm background helped in this regard. Although Blanchard continued working with the insurance company, Henrietta initially devoted all her time to the care of her family.

In 1942, Henrietta gave birth to a third child, a daughter whom she and Blanchard named Henrietta. By this time her husband, who had studied to be a steam boiler operator at the Camden County Vocational and Technical School, in Pennsauken, New Jersey, was employed at Fort Dix Army Base, in Wrightstown, New Jersey, as a fireman. He held this position for thirty years before retiring.

Not long after moving to the country, Henrietta resumed working as a musician. Her return to work began a period, lasting almost fifty years, that was the most productive of her life. Down to the mid 1980s, Henrietta was a veritable whirlwind, a person with great energy and strong leadership skills, and one who engaged in, often simultaneously, multiple musical activities.

In 1937, Henrietta started giving private lessons to piano students, in due time securing eight or nine pupils. She also found other work in the community. When Blanchard and she joined St. John's Methodist Church in nearby Berlin, the church needed an organist-choir director. Henrietta took the job. At the same time, Blanchard became the church's assistant pastor.

Henrietta carried out a variety of musical activities at St. John's. Each Sunday she played for the worship service, directed the Senior Choir, and played for the Sunday School. She used hymns from the Methodist Episcopal hymnal and whatever gospel music was popular at the time. While serving as organist-choir director, Henrietta also combined the work of the church with her private music practice, by holding concerts and recitals at the church.

As another part of her musical activities, Henrietta assisted area churches with their music programs. Located in places such as Blackwood, Mt. Holly, Burlington, Camden, and Vineland, most were affiliates of the AME, Methodist, or Methodist Episcopal conferences. Through this work, she befriended a number of fine church musicians. Ruth Roberts Worthington, the organist-choir director of the Mount Zion AME Church in Kresson, part of Voorhees Township, was one close associate. When she started playing at Mt. Zion, Ruth accompanied the church's youth choir, directed by Stanley Ambrose, a musician who lived in West Berlin whom Henrietta also knew. A great vocalist, choir director, guitarist, pianist, and composer,

13

he traveled with his ensembles giving concerts throughout the region. Publishing two gospel hymns, *Somewhere There Is A City* (1931), and *I Have a Home* (1931), he sold them piece by piece.

Still another musician whom Henrietta met was Laura Beeks Outlaw, a very talented pianist who played for the Greengrove Baptist Church in Berlin as a teenager and young adult. Their most important association came later, in the 1970's, when both served as officers of the Marian Anderson Music Guild, Camden Chapter of the National Association for Negro Musicians, in the 1970's. While Henrietta was president, Laura, who had lived in New York City for more than twenty years before returning to southern New Jersey, was the group's treasurer. Henrietta also worked with Laura's successor at Greengrove Baptist Church, Almeda Woods Taylor, a young woman who was organist at the church for at least fifteen or twenty years.

Eventually Henrietta's church work led her to a local community center, the West Atco Improvement League. Many of the church people and community people attended its programs. Henrietta worked at the Improvement League with her friend, Amy Edwards, who was the secretary of the organization. Originally from Philadelphia, she was a graduate of Shippensburg State College and a school teacher. Amy's husband, a veteran of the Spanish American War, was the League's president. Inspired by the work of Marcus Garvey, they organized this community center to encourage people to improve themselves by engaging in cultural and entrepreneurial activities.

Henrietta taught a music class for children at the Improvement League on Friday afternoons for about ten years. Periodically during the year, she also presented her students in recitals and concerts there. At one Improvement League concert, held June 9, 1962, Henrietta included her brother Raymond on the program, and sang four mezzo-soprano selections.

Unable to attend meetings of the Philadelphia Music Teachers Association, Henrietta joined the South Jersey Music Teachers Association in the early 1940s. Most of its meetings were in Haddonfield at the First United Methodist Church at Warwick Road and Kings Highway. By attending the meetings, she kept up with the trends in teaching. On occasion, Henrietta invited a colleague from the association to lecture on the importance of music at her recitals. When a member wrote a book, she would buy it to show to her students.

Always busy combining her interests in music, church, and working with young people, Henrietta started another project in the early 1950s. She decided to help her niece, Annabelle Ridley,

Henrietta, pictured with several students from her piano class at the West Atco Improvement League, in Atco, New Jersey, beams proudly at the conclusion of a recital. Circa 1950's. Photo courtesy of H. F. Robinson.

and her niece's husband, Thomas Ridley, both students at the Manna Bible Institute in Philadelphia, with their missionary work by operating a Christian camp on her farm. To learn how to set up a camp, Henrietta took a correspondence course from the Moody Bible Institute in Chicago. Her brother Hercules, who was visiting from California, suggested that she name the camp Robinson's Oak Farm because of the oak trees on her property. Because she thought that this name was too long, Henrietta herself decided to use the name Robin Oaks Farm. To advertise she had a brochure printed with photographs of the students and teachers, a list of camp activities, and an application form.

Henrietta opened the Robin Oaks Farm Christian Camp in July 1952. Although she was the camp director, she cooked all the meals and played music for the services. Henrietta started the morning by playing opening exercises. Then she carried out her kitchen chores. In the evening she played for the evening-song service.

In the first year, Henrietta put the children in two unused bedrooms in her house. The next year, her son Alonzo built a little cabin and a chapel from cement block; she housed the boys in the cabin, while keeping the girls in the house. Charging ten dollars a week, Henrietta usually had ten students enrolled each month. She ran the camp in July and August from 1952 to 1956.

In 1959, after working for twenty-two years at St. John's Methodist Church, Henrietta left, prompted by changes in the church's administration. She soon started another job playing for the West Atco's Calvary Baptist Church. Leaving St. John's for the same reason, Blanchard became assistant pastor of St. Mary's Methodist Church in Burlington, New Jersey.

While she played some music from the Baptist hymnal at West Atco's Calvary Baptist Church, Henrietta played mostly gospel music, the music of individuals such as Thomas Dorsey, Lucie Campbell, Clara Ward, and Gertrude Ward. As soon as the leading songs from Chicago and Philadelphia were published, selections such as *He Knows How Much You Can Bear* and *I'll Fly Away,* Henrietta purchased the sheet music from the gospel music store in Philadelphia.

Besides playing for the choir, Henrietta made robes for the twelve members of the West Atco Calvary Baptist Church. She had made choir robes before, since her mother, a dressmaker, taught her to sew as a child. Also, after moving to the country, Henrietta studied dressmaking and tailoring at a Singer Sewing Center nearby. This enabled her to earn additional income by making clothes for various white women in the area.

During her second year at the West Atco Calvary Baptist Church, despite Henrietta's preference for country living, her husband decided they should move back to the city. Keeping their property in Evesham Township for Blanchard's real estate business, they bought a house in Camden, at 208 Federal Street. When they moved in 1960, Henrietta left her job at the West Atco Calvary Baptist Church. Blanchard resigned his position at St. Mary's Church, retired from the ministry, then joined Tindley Temple Methodist Church in Philadelphia.

Shortly after moving to Camden, Henrietta took another job with a country church. This was the Antioch Christian Community Church, on the White Horse Pike in Chesilhurst. It was a small church with few children, but it was very pleasant and Henrietta was very good friends with the pastor, Reverend Mattie Dodson. She remained its organist for eight years.

Henrietta continued giving private music lessons and student recitals. Having access to transportation, six of her students from Berlin came to the city for their lessons. Gradually, other students came and her enrollment grew. For her lessons, Henrietta rented a music studio at the YWCA, at 565 Stevens Street, which had several rooms with pianos. She presented her recitals in the auditorium at the "Y" and in the auditorium at Rutgers University for recitals.

To earn other income, Henrietta taught in the Camden public schools. She became a substitute teacher, and taught reading and math. In the schools she met many youths who needed additional help, so she tutored them in their academic subjects, carrying out this work for about ten years.

For many years on Saturday mornings, Henrietta also taught individuals and groups at the YWCA. At home in the evenings she taught adults. Between the "Y" and her home, Henrietta taught thirty-five students a week.

Some of Henrietta's students studied with her for several years. A number of the children were very talented and they became professional musicians. One was Rachel Merrill, who studied with Henrietta for three years and became the organist of the Mission Evangelistic Church in Camden. Her father, Reverend Merrill, who founded the church, had attended the Manna Bible School and worked at the Robin Oaks Christian Camp. Some of Henrietta's other students studied with her for four or five years, then continued studying with other music teachers. Henrietta was always very proud later to see former students directing choirs and playing for churches.

Henrietta kept abreast of her music studies by attending various courses. Quite often she went to study with Frances Clark, who had been her instructor in the WPA training program at the Settlement Music School. Besides directing the New School for Music in Princeton, Clark was associated with Westminster Choir College. Her curriculum was for anyone interested in teaching and Henrietta studied Modern Theory, Improvisation, Advanced Repertoire, Piano Pedagogy, History of Music, and Techniques for Performance. Frances Clark's book, *Time To Begin*, she used when teaching very little children. Besides attending the New School for Music, Henrietta went to seminars conducted by music publishers. She also received a Choral Conductor's Certificate from the Chicago Conservatory and a Piano Teacher's Certificate from the U.S. School of Music in New York City.

Along with teaching and playing music, writing children's works and lyrics also interested Henrietta and she produced two publications. The first was a coloring book for children entitled, *Stories of New Jersey*, that was published in 1962. In 1964, in association with the Walt Whitman Association, she wrote a brief illustrated history of New Jersey, titled *My Jerseyland*. In 1981, Henrietta wrote and

obtained a copyright for a song, *My Jerseyland, A Prayer For Our State.*
She first set her lyric to the tune of the familiar Christmas song, *O Tannenbaum.* Then Henrietta sent it to a commercial song writing company, which set her lyric to the tune of the song *Oh Maryland.*

Over time Henrietta expanded her activities at the YWCA. Since she was there each week teaching music, the board of directors recruited her to work with them. Henrietta thus served on the board for six years. With other mothers she also worked in the Student Aid Club, while Jean Moorer served as its president. Each Saturday the club members tutored children in their school work. They also took the children on several bus trips throughout New Jersey to teach them more about history and sponsored fundraising events to raise money to give scholarships. While working at the "Y", Henrietta continued to emphasize student recitals and other musical programs. Parents, friends and board members helped sponsor the events, which she customarily staged in the "Y" auditorium. Henrietta produced and promoted the concerts and recitals as the Robinson Studios.

In the recitals, Henrietta fostered her students' interest in music performance by inviting guest artists to play. Fabian Hunter, a well-known Camden pianist, and Rhonda Jones, a vocalist, were two artists that Henrietta featured at the "Y". Her nephew, Robert Houston, also performed as a magician. Henrietta gave a concert every February during Negro History Month to promote black music.

For several years, Henrietta presented a monthly program at the YWCA called the *Amateur Hour.* It was for musicians of all ages throughout the city, not just her students. The participants performed on a variety of instruments or sang; on two separate occasions, Henrietta's daughter sang, and her granddaughter Celeste played the clarinet. Although judges for the *Amateur Hour* awarded special prizes for the best performances, they gave certificates to all the children who participated in the program.

Area music teachers enthusiastically supported Henrietta's work at the "Y," working with her as part of an informal association of music professionals. The teachers entered their students in her recitals and performed as guest artists in her concerts. Dr. Edward Fraction, a respected member of the Music Department at Camden High School, was one such teacher. Henrietta knew his mother, having taught her in the first grade at the Elk Township School near Glassboro. Emily Lucken Brown was another top music teacher who helped. Besides teaching, she played for a popular radio program on WKDN radio station in Camden, called the *Kershaw Hour* (later *Words and Music.*) A sensational musician and teacher, Roberta Holmes, also supported Henrietta's "Y" recitals.

WHY ???   *THE AMATEUR*   HOUR ???

THE OBJECT OF THE CAMDEN

AMATEUR HOUR

IS TO GIVE MUSIC STUDENTS AN OPPORTUNITY TO PERFORM. IT
IS EVERY THIRD SATURDAY P. M. MANY FEEL THERE IS NO POINT
IN PRACTICING HIS LESSON WHEN THERE IS NO CHANCE TO
PLAY, EXCEPT AT AN ANNUAL RECITAL.

AMATEUR HOUR is available several times a year for any
student from First Book on, when the teacher sponsors him.

Students spurt like magic when they sign up to be on the
AMATEUR HOUR . . . and practice like mad, with joy and
excitement.

PRIZES — Are Gifts from Local Commercial Businesses.

REQUIREMENTS — Any kind of talent may enter. No age limit.

JUDGES — Closed ballot of each one in the listening audience.

WINNERS — Are announced on Radio Program, and Awards are made the
following third Saturday.

FINALE — Each monthly winner will compete in Spring Concert.

ANYBODY — Anyone who does not care to compete, can be given opportunity to "do their thing" of first part of program. No age limit.

*This is NOT a Federal Program. It is based by conscientious music lovers,
parents and music teachers, who want the Youth to have proper outlet for
performance and inspiration.*

EXECUTIVE COMMITTEE	SPONSORS
MRS. EMILY L. BROWN	ST. JOSEPH'S GIFT SHOP
MRS. ETHEL HOUSTON	DAN'S ONE-HOUR DRY CLEANER
MRS. NAOMI MERRILL	SUBURBAN ENTERPRISES (Cosmetics)
MRS. GLADYS STILL	SMITH & HOUSTON, Plumbers
MRS. EMMA WILSON	CAMDEN MODELLING SCHOOL
MRS. H. F. ROBINSON, *Chairman*	

ENTRY BLANK: Include Name, Address, Act, also Teacher's Signature,
Address, Phone, etc.

MAIL TO: AMATEUR HOUR, c/o Robinson Studio
439 Broadway, Camden, N. J. 08103

*Directing the Amateur Hour, and other community center programs, was a
hallmark of Henrietta's work in southern New Jersey. She designed and first
distributed this leaflet advertisement in the 1960's. Courtesy H. F. Robinson.*

After she stopped playing for Antioch Christian Community Church in 1968, Henrietta joined the Broadway United Methodist Church in Camden. Then she and her husband decided to move from Second and Federal Streets to 439 Broadway in Camden, because they thought the area was safer. Henrietta and Blanchard purchased a storefront. Her husband used it for his real estate business, which supplemented his work at Fort Dix. She set up Robinson Studio of Music, with a few keyboard instruments. In the mid 1970s, after crime increased in this neighborhood, Henrietta and Blanchard sold their storefront and moved again, to Northgate Apartments at Seventh and Linden Streets in Camden. After they moved, Henrietta stopped teaching her Saturday morning piano class at the YWCA. However, she continued giving private lessons in her home,

Henrietta's student, Allison Wilson, during a lesson at the Robinson Studio of Music, 439 Federal Street in Camden, in the early 1970's. Courtesy H. F. Robinson.

working as a pianist-organist by accompanying choirs or substituting at churches, and presenting concerts and recitals at the "Y".

In the spring of 1977, Camden vocalist Isabelle Collins performed at Henrietta's YWCA concert. Isabelle was a very active singer and music teacher, who as a young woman had also studied with Marian Anderson. For many years she gave concerts throughout the United States, Canada, the Caribbean, and Europe. Although her repertoire included French, Italian, and German songs, she sang Negro spirituals more than any other music.

After her Spring 1977 performance, Isabelle Collins asked Henrietta to join the Camden Chapter of the National Association of Negro Musicians (NANM). It was an affiliate of NANM's national organization, founded in 1919 by the upper echelon of black musicians and based in Chicago. She and Reverend J. Ferman Little, also a musician and pastor of the First Church of God on Walnut Street in Camden, had founded the chapter in 1971. Initially eight or nine people became members and they met at Reverend Little's church. Soon there were over twenty members.

Because of their mutual interests, Isabelle Collins thought that Henrietta should work with the Camden Chapter of NANM. Henrietta agreed with Isabelle's idea. In November of the same year, they co-sponsored a concert at the "Y" and joined the Camden Chapter of NANM. Diligently working to fulfill its mission, the chapter encouraged young people who studied classical or church music to become professional musicians, and promoted the music of African American composers.

After joining NANM, Henrietta was immediately elected president of the chapter. Serving in that capacity, she prepared a "year" book with the chapter's annual program schedule and the members' names and addresses, obtained volunteers to chair events, and organized work committees. She also directed the chapter's Negro History Month program, since she had given similar programs at the YWCA annually. Henrietta always included some history about Negro composers in these programs. Each year at the chapter's anniversary banquet, she also honored members who had worked faithfully in music and made outstanding contributions to the chapter.

By this time, many of Henrietta's friends and peers were active members of the Camden Chapter of NANM. They were primarily music teachers, church organists, and choir directors: Ruth Worthington, Roberta Holmes, Essie Holmes Voorhees, Laura Outlaw, Reverend Mattie Dodson, Emily Lucken Brown, Lottie James, Alberta Johnson, Esau O'Neal, Gladys Still, and Dorothy Conley.

Working on the chapter's Youth Committee, Henrietta and other members planned benefit concerts to raise money for students, whenever possible obtaining free use of the Walt Whitman Center for the Arts or other places in Camden and the area. Successful in this endeavor, they were able to make contributions to NANM's national

21

scholarship fund each year. (The singers Marian Anderson, Grace Bumbry, and Jessye Norman are among those who have won NANM's scholarships in the past.) Henrietta and the members also presented small scholarships to one or two local students who attended college.

Henrietta enjoyed attending NANM's national conventions and regional meetings, which were usually held in the cities with the largest membership, such as New York, Los Angeles, St. Louis, and Denver. Through the years she has worked on some of the convention committees, including the Time and Place Committee and the Scholarship Committee. Because of her work with NANM, on November 13, 1982, at its Annual Founder's Day Luncheon, the Eastern Region of NANM, of which the Camden Chapter is a part, honored Henrietta for her contribution and service in the field of music and presented her with a plaque. Chaired by Mercedes M. Keeler, the luncheon was at the Bellevue Stratford Hotel in Philadelphia. NANM's national president Betty Jackson King, who was a very dynamic music teacher living in Wildwood, New Jersey, and Robert Henson, who was the Eastern Region Director, were both present.

Although other organizations had given her awards before, Henrietta was especially pleased to be recognized by NANM for her work in music. Such recognition, as well as other awards, justified her struggle to help people and encouraged her to continue working.

One of Henrietta's most memorable experiences occurred in 1982, while she was president of the Camden Chapter of NANM. Since other chapters were already named after prominent musicians, such as Roland Hayes and R. Nathaniel Dett, that year Henrietta wrote to her former teacher, Marian Anderson, asking for permission to rename the chapter after Miss Anderson. In a letter dated June 15, 1982, Marian Anderson replied and gave her consent. From that time the chapter became officially, the Marian Anderson Guild, Camden Chapter of the National Association of Negro Musicians. Henrietta was president of the chapter for ten years.

Henrietta's work with NANM prompted her to undertake a very special project that was funded by the New Jersey Historical Commission. In 1983, she began to research the lives of many of her associates to compile their biographies and write a history of black musicians in southern New Jersey.

In 1986, Henrietta began to scale back her activities, including her work with NANM, to care for her husband, who had become seriously ill. Blanchard died in 1990. After his death, Henrietta, hoping to publish her research, resumed work on her history of black musicians in southern New Jersey; completing her manuscript, she called it *The Forgotten Music Teacher*. She also, heeding the advice of

The Twenty-fifth Anniversary celebration of the Marian Anderson Music Guild, Camden Chapter of the National Association of Negro Musicians, held May 18, 1996 at Grace Temple Baptist Church in Lawnside, New Jersey, was an especially joyous occasion for Henrietta Fuller Robinson, who was honored for her superb ten years as its president.

Foreground, left to right: Arzulia O'Neal, fourth chapter president; Carolyn Willis; Henrietta Fuller Robinson, second chapter president; Teresa Epps. Back row, left to right: Carol Wims; Rachel Merrill, newly elected and fifth chapter president (and Henrietta's former student); Esau O'Neal, third chapter president; Constance Hampton; Mary O. Robinson; Martha Morton. Not pictured, Isabelle Crews Collins, co-founder; Rev. J. Ferman Little, co-founder and first president. Photograph by C. C. Williams.

Frances Clark, did not retire from her music career altogether. Rather, she played for a chorus in her apartment building, chaired programs for the Marian Anderson Guild, and taught privately.

Although Henrietta continued to teach, each year she had fewer students, especially children between the ages of ten and fourteen. Some children started to study, then losing interest, quit after three or four lessons. Most children were not interested. Henrietta found that the popularity of recorded music and television contributed to their lack of interest. Later she saw that changes in the schools also had an effect. In schools in the past, there were always two or three children in every class who played the piano. The teachers would call on them to perform in concerts and thereby enhance their interest in music. However with increased crime, drug use, and budget problems, many schools eliminated music programs completely. Henrietta was very concerned about the lack of interest and support for music education in the community.

To keep working, Henrietta focused on giving lessons to preschool children and senior citizens. Her program for preschoolers was called "Musical Kindergarten". For the senior citizens, all who had studied music as children and wanted to play again, Henrietta wrote her own music book. It included *Come Thou Fount, Blessed Assurance, Just As I Am, Amen, There's A Bright Side Somewhere, Sweet Hour of Prayer, When the Saints Come Marching In,* and *Happy Birthday.* She transposed all but two pieces into the key of "C", so that her students did not have to play many sharp and flat notes.

Looking back at her achievements, Henrietta was pleased with her involvement in music throughout her life. She was thankful that her mother sang hymns to their family, and gave them music lessons. Furthermore, Henrietta was gratified that she continued to study music, to maintain her expertise, and adapt to the changing times. Whether she worked as a music teacher, pianist, organist, choir director, or talent promoter, she eagerly faced the challenge. Indeed, although she never made much money, Henrietta thoroughly enjoyed working as a professional musician.

Henrietta dedicated her time and energy to instill the love of music in her students, their families, and in the community at large. She was delighted by her students, and was pleased that some of them became professional musicians. Henrietta believed fundamentally, and often stated: "Music is a wonderful thing. You just can't live without it." Knowing that its appeal is universal, she is pleased to have been a part of that universe. That is her assessment of her long and productive life.

AFTERWORD

In her ninetieth decade, Henrietta carried on her work as a music teacher in her home in Camden. She taught piano students: three preschoolers, two older children, one middle-aged adult, and four senior citizens. One of the children, Richard Saunders, was an exceptionally fine young musician. Presenting her students in recital twice a year, Henrietta continued giving lessons through the early spring of 1996. Such dedication, indeed, confirmed her life long regard for music.

A brief profile of Henrietta's life was published in two books by Dr. Rebecca Batts Butler: *Profiles of outstanding Blacks in South Jersey during the 1950's, 1960's, 1970's,* Reynolds Publishers, 1980; *Portraits of Black Role Models in the History of Southern New Jersey,* Acme Craftsmen Publishers, 1985. Prominent as an educator in southern New Jersey, Dr. Butler was a notable member of the South Jersey Chapter of the Association for the Study of Afro-American Life and History, that sponsored publication of her biographical studies.

PART TWO

African American Church Musicians and Music Teachers in Southern New Jersey, 1915-1990

A Biographical Dictionary

ABBREVIATIONS

AME African Methodist Episcopal

AMEZ African Methodist Episcopal Zion

ASALH Association for the Study of Afro-American
Life and History

AUMP African Union Methodist Protestant

CME Christian Methodist Episcopal

ME Methodist Episcopal

NAACP National Association for the Advancement of Colored
People

NANM National Association of Negro Musicians

SDA Seventh-day Adventist

UAME Union African Methodist Episcopal

WPA Works Progress Administration

YMCA Young Men's Christian Association

YWCA Young Women's Christian Association

ALLISON, THEODORA M. (b. 1900), pianist, organist, music teacher. Theodora, the eldest of the two children of Theodore and Gertrude (Thomas) Hayes, was born at 707 Cherry Street in Camden, New Jersey on August 6, 1900. A porter on the railroad who worked frequently away from home, Theodora's father and namesake was born in Tennessee in 1873. Her mother, an accomplished musician whom she would later emulate, was born in Camden in 1878. The Hayes' youngest child, two years younger than Theodora, was her brother Alfred Leslie. Throughout her childhood, Theodora's family lived in Camden with her mother's parents, David and Phillis Thomas. A cousin, Eva Miller, eleven years older and like a sister to Theodora, also grew up in the household. Deeply religious, the Hayes and Thomas families worshipped at Macedonia AME Church in Camden.

Educated in the public schools of Camden, Theodora entered the Mt. Vernon Public School, a segregated grammar school, in the fall of 1906. In 1914, Theodora's formal education ended with her graduation from eighth grade. Having transferred a few years earlier, Theodora completed her schooling at the John Greenleaf Whittier Grammar School. Like Mt. Vernon, Whittier was a segregated school.

From infancy, Theodora was exposed to religious music by her mother, a dedicated church musician who had studied privately and excelled as a pianist and vocalist. Whenever her mother rehearsed or entertained their family, she learned to sing hymns and Negro spirituals. Also a popular concert artist, Theodora's mother, and her mother's sister, Selena (Thomas) Miller, a talented vocalist, performed frequently at many churches in southern New Jersey. Tragically, on Sunday October 26, 1906, while traveling to give a concert in Atlantic City, both died in the infamous Pennsylvania Railroad's "Disaster at Thorofare Swingbridge" train wreck. (Shortly after 2 P.M., the electric train plunged off the Thorofare drawbridge into the Atlantic City bay: 56 of the 96 occupants on board, primarily women and children, drowned.)

In the year immediately following her mother's death, Theodora showed a serious interest in playing the piano. She was six years old and had just started attending school. By the time she was seven, her grandparents, having primary responsibility for raising her and her brother, arranged for Bella Morris to give her lessons in their home. Addressed as Madame Morris, she was their church's organist, as well as a prominent teacher. For three or four years, Theodora studied basic theory, religious music, and classical compositions. Providing her with an excellent foundation, these lessons were her only formal music instruction. Self-taught thereafter, Theodora easily mastered challenging compositions that she performed by memory.

As she made the transition from student to church musician and performer, using her talent at Macedonia AME Church helped to foster Theodora's interest in music. At age twelve, Theodora, who also sang in the youth choir, started to play for her church's Sunday school. Earning a reputation as an accomplished musician within a year, she was soon sought after to play in other venues.

Theodora's professional career started when she was thirteen, and in her final year at grammar school. Hearing of her talent, the manager of the Lyric Theater, a moving picture theater located at Newton Avenue and Broadway in Camden, offered her a job playing piano during the screening of silent movies. With her grandparents' permission, Theodora accepted the work, finding it an exciting way to earn money. For the next two years, Theodora played each weekend, as a result gaining valuable seasoning as a pianist.

While still in her early teens, Theodora became the accompanist of a choir that was an outgrowth of the Sunday School Choir at Camden's Wesley AMEZ Church. She was recruited to this position by a childhood associate, Rose (Payne) Wilson, who was a prominent member of the church, and the founder and director of both ensembles. The young people gave afternoon or evening concerts at various churches throughout the city. Playing for the choir afforded Theodora the opportunity to perform as a solo artist on several occasions.

At a social given by a fellow chorister, Theodora was introduced to James R. Allison, of West Cape May, New Jersey. She was fourteen and he was twenty-three. After a three month, whirlwind courtship, they were married at Macedonia AME Church on August 8, 1915, two days after Theodora's fifteenth birthday. Settling into married life in West Cape May, the young couple had four children, born between 1916 and 1921; from eldest to youngest they were James Jr., Theodore, Juanita, and Warren. After her grandfather's death, Theodora's grandmother Phillis also lived with them.

By teaching piano in her home, Theodora quickly established her reputation as a fine musician in the Cape May community. Her students included her own children; James Jr., upholding the family tradition, established an equally noteworthy career. After Theodora's instruction, he studied with a Roman Catholic sister, then secured a position playing for Wesley AMEZ Church in Camden, at age sixteen. While in the military during World War II, he served as an organist-choir director. When he returned to civilian life, James Jr. resumed playing for Wesley, took positions at other area churches, and worked as a music therapist. Mary (Edmonds) Burrell, another of Theodora's talented students, became a fine pianist and later, the director of the Women's Choir at Kaighn Avenue Baptist Church in Camden.

Shortly after moving to West Cape May, Theodora and her husband converted to Christian Science, and joined Cape May City's First Church of Christ Scientist. Membership in the church marked the start of Theodora's forty plus years of work as a church organist, serving full time at her church, and substituting at the First Church of Christ Scientist in Wildwood. Because the churches did not have choirs, her work entailed playing for the order of service, and accompanying vocal soloists.

During the early 1920's, Theodora, because of her reputation, was offered a position playing the piano at the Liberty Theater, a moving picture theater in Cape May City. It was owned and operated by a father and son team, immigrants from Germany. Since she had enjoyed this line of work as a teenager and the pay was generous, Theodora, by then in her early twenties, accepted the job. Her employers were soon confronted by individuals from the white community who, in support of racial segregation, objected to her working there; the owner and his son ignored the complaints. After installing a pipe organ in the theater, they selected Theodora, the best musician among their six female employees, to play it. Although not previously schooled on the instrument, a week of instruction by the manager, combined with her disciplined practice, was sufficient for her to play adeptly. As the organist, Theodora rehearsed and performed for the vaudeville acts booked into the theater. A notable achievement in her work at the Liberty Theater was her improvisation of background music for various performances, necessitated by the entertainers lack of musical scores. In fact, many patrons of the theater, marveling at her skill, often complimented her and asked what conservatory had she attended. Theodora always replied: "I didn't attend any music school. Except for lessons with a teacher when I was a child, I am a self-taught musician."

Eventually, Theodora and her husband moved to a home on Lafayette Street in Cape May. At that time, she became the accompanist of a local women's chorus directed by Helen Ball, a city resident. The inter-racial group, consisting of fifteen to twenty women, performed classical and secular choral music, primarily at community events and special holiday programs. From time to time, Theodora also presented her own compositions, *Cape May Blues* and *Smiling Eyes,* a blues tune and a love ballad, respectively. Composed in the 1930's when her children were in high school, *Cape May Blues* included a lyric written by her husband. Reading a poem in the *Evening Bulletin,* a newspaper published in Philadelphia, Pennsylvania, inspired Theodora to write *Smiling Eyes.*

In the early 1960's because her husband was not well, Theodora retired as the organist of the First Church of Christ Scientist in Cape May. During the next twenty years, living alternately in Camden for ten years and Cape May for another ten, Theodora did not accept any formal position as a musician. However, she played for her own pleasure.

By 1981, Theodora and James Sr. left Cape May a second time. They built a small apartment onto their youngest son's home in Pennsauken, New Jersey, and moved into it. At that time, she and her husband joined the First Church of Christ Scientist in Moorestown. When the church's organist retired, Theodora started to play for services, ending her twenty year hiatus from work as a church musician. She served four years as organist, until her husband's death in 1986. From 1986 to 1991, Theodora remained semi-retired, playing as needed for a Christian Science retirement home in Baltimore, Maryland, where she briefly resided, and the First Church of Christ Scientist in Moorestown.

Eventually settling into an apartment in Somerdale, New Jersey, Theodora accepted a full-time position as organist of the First Church of Christ Scientist in Haddon Heights, a town nearby, at age ninety-two. Remarkably, through the benefits of her good health and her incredible dedication, she has not retired and still functions in this post.

AMBROSE, STANLEY G. (1887-196?), vocalist, pianist, guitarist, music teacher, choral director, composer. Stanley, born in Chester Township (later Moorestown), New Jersey in 1887, was the youngest child of George and Catharine (née ?) Ambrose. They had seven children, in order by age, between the years 1870 and 1887: Olivia, Lillian, Viola, Elizabeth, Martha, Daniel, and Stanley. While the eldest was born in Pennsylvania, the younger children were born in New Jersey, in Mt. Laurel and Chester.

A native of New Jersey, Stanley's mother was born in 1848. She died sometime before his tenth birthday. His father was born in Pennsylvania in 1845. After the family moved to Chester Township, he supported them by working in a brick mill. Notably, in 1882, George Ambrose, who was also a respected minister, founded a mission in a local hall that eventually became the Bethel AME Church of Moorestown. (In recognition of his role as founder and forty-one years of service, the church awarded him a gold medal on November 23, 1923.) Since his father re-married in 1898, Stanley was partially raised by his stepmother, Mary (Bridley) Ambrose, along with her daughter from her first marriage, Florence Bridley. Also outliving Mary, his father married a third wife, Bennie, between 1911 and 1920.

When Stanley was born, the Ambrose family lived at 550 North Church Road. Educated in the public schools, he attended School Number Seven, a segregated grammar school located in the 400 Block of North Church. Whether he obtained a secondary school education is unknown.

From the time he was a small child, music was an important part of Stanley's life. Musically talented themselves, his mother and father taught their children to sing in harmony. This early vocal training enhanced Stanley's natural abilities and fostered his interest in playing musical instruments. Since the Ambrose family had a piano, it was the first instrument he learned to play. Like other boys his age, Stanley also loved to strum the guitar. Self-taught, he became proficient enough to teach others.

Bethel AME Church, where his father served as both pastor and later, assistant pastor, was located in the same block of North Church as their home. Recognized for their fine musical talent, the Ambrose children were active members of the church's choir. Although physically small in stature, even as an adult, Stanley was very robust, and had a tremendous, booming voice. Because of his powerful singing, he became a song leader during services.

By the time he was a teenager, Stanley began to perform at area churches. As he grew older, his voice deepened into a distinctive double bass that amazed all who heard him. Accompanying himself on the guitar, Stanley sang inspiring renditions of hymns, and Negro spirituals. Besides performing as a soloist, he organized and directed small choral groups, consisting of other young people from his church. At times, he played the piano for nearby churches.

Leaving home sometime before his twenty-first birthday, Stanley went to live with his sisters, Lillian and Martha, who had rented a house at 12 Beech Street, just two streets from their father's home. Martha was married to Frederick Blake, an ice cream manufacturer.

While earning a living working at odd jobs, Stanley devoted his life to music. To enhance his conducting skills, he traveled to Philadelphia, Pennsylvania, and Camden, New Jersey, to attend concerts given by leading black musicians and church choirs of the day. In addition, Stanley maintained a close association with his brother Daniel, who directed Bethel AME's choir and later became the choir director of a church in Pennsauken, New Jersey, and Peter French, the organist and a trustee of their church. Both talented and respected musicians, they were addressed as "Professor" by members of the community. By keeping abreast of new music and techniques and through the influences of his brother and French, Stanley developed a unique style of teaching, conducting, and arranging music.

Serving in the army during World War I, Stanley, who was nearly thirty years old, was shipped overseas to Europe. His exposure to mustard gas while in the service partially disabled him, allowing him to collect a military pension. After his discharge, Stanley returned home and went to work for a contractor.

By 1920, the house on Beech Street was filled with more Ambrose family members. Stanley's sister Martha had a daughter, Marie, who was one and a half years old. His sister Viola, Viola's husband John Dean, and his sister Olivia's son, Albert Quann, had also moved there. After a few years, Stanley decided to move himself. In the mid 1920's, he settled further down in the country, living with other relatives in West Berlin, a part of Voorhees Township.

After moving, Stanley had more opportunities to work as a musician than he had when living in Chester Township, where there were several experienced musicians, including his brother. Although the black population was very small, there were four black churches in the vicinity. Stanley joined Mt. Zion AME Church, located on Route 73 in the Kresson section of Voorhees. Founded as the People's Church of Milford in 1800, it reportedly was first served by AME ministers in 1848.

Because he loved working with children, Stanley organized a youth choir at Mt. Zion AME Church. Known throughout the area as the Kresson Choir, they sang for Sunday worship and performed at area churches during fellowship. To introduce his choral members to the best music of the era, Stanley took them to concerts, locally and in the nearby cities. A few of the youngsters that he taught to play the guitar accompanied the choir. Also featuring talented soloists in his choral arrangements, Stanley coached several young singers, including Chester Worthington, Roy Forman, Helen Forman, and Cora Macklin. The choir's fiery performances drew large audiences that filled the country churches to capacity. Under his direction for over ten years, the Kresson Choir's repertoire consisted of Methodist hymns, Negro spirituals, gospel hymns, and hymns that Stanley composed.

In 1931, Stanley, obtaining copyrights to at least two of his original compositions written in the genre of early gospel hymns, published them in collaboration with Francis Alfred Clark. A resident of Philadelphia, Pennsylvania, Clark was an outstanding musician, composer, and arranger, who had collaborated on several hymns with Reverend Charles Albert Tindley, one of the earliest creators of gospel music. After composing the lyrics and melodies to *Somewhere There Is A City* and *I Have A Home*, Stanley engaged Clark to prepare the harmony and arrangements. Then he sold or presented copies to his students, other musicians, and church members.

By the early 1930's, Stanley, who had moved to a house on Cooper Road in Berlin, was very popular with the youngsters in his neighborhood. Generous to a fault, he bought bicycles, and other toys for a number of children. He entertained them, by telling wonderful stories, creating beautiful sketches and paintings, and taking them on trips to the zoo. Since Stanley's greatest pleasure was his music, he also started teaching many of them to sing and play the guitar.

Using four of his most talented pupils, Stanley formed a male quartet that he called the Berlin Junior Harmony Four. Between the ages of ten and twelve, the members were Elijah Brown, Albert Hudson, Eugene Jeter-Bey, and William Jordan. To provide accompaniment for the group, Stanley trained Albert to play the guitar. In preparing them to perform in public, Stanley often took the quartet to hear other singers, as he had his youth choir members. One of the most memorable trips that he organized was to Philadelphia's Convention Hall, for the appearance of Wings Over Jordan, the renowned radio broadcast choir of Gethsemane Church in Cleveland, Ohio. Because of his great commitment to teaching, Stanley was very successful in fostering his students interest in music.

On one occasion, while Stanley and the quartet attended evening fellowship at a church in Albion, the scheduled performers failed to arrive. Taking advantage of the opportunity, Stanley arranged for the Berlin Junior Harmony Four to sing as replacements. Performing before many of their relatives and neighbors for the first time, they thrilled the crowd with a spirited presentation. After their successful premiere, Stanley traveled with the quartet throughout southern New

SOMEWHERE

Words and Music by Stanley G. I. Ambrose

Harmonized and Arr. by F. A. Clark

1. Some-where there is a cit - y, The streets are pav'd with gold,
2. If you would reach that cit - y, That lies be-yond the sea,
3. Some-where your Moth-er's look - ing, To see her chil-dren dear,
4. Some-where a voice is call - ing, I hear it sweet and clear,

Its walls are all of jas - per, Its wealth (Its wealth) un - told. (un - told.)
Je - sus somewhere is wait - ing, He died for thee.
Some-where be - yond old Jor - dan, Some-where, some- where.
It is the Sav-iour's plead - ing, I know He's near.

CHORUS

Some-where we'll meet up yon- der, Je - sus, yes, He will be there,

And we'll sing and shout, all glo - ry, Some-where, some-where.
Somewhere, somewhere.

Self-published, and composing in the tradition of early twentieth century African American gospel hymn writers, Ambrose sold his sheet music to his students and associates. Courtesy of Albert Hudson. Reprinted by permission of Marie Blake, (deceased).

Ambrose, recognized for his unique harmonies and phrasing, favored guitar accompaniment in his choral arrangements. His great influence was evident in the performances of a number of vocalists in Voorhees, Berlin, and other southern New Jersey communities, well into the 1990's. See photo credit previous page.

Jersey. Since singing with amplification had come into fashion, Stanley, who was attentive to every detail, also taught them to sing with microphones, which they first did at a church in Atlantic City. Performing together into the early 1940's, the group disbanded as the young men either entered the military, or married.

In his early fifties at that time, Stanley essentially retired from choral directing. However, he never stopped teaching music or appearing as an impromptu soloist. On Sundays, he continued his custom of visiting different congregations. Honored by his presence, the pastors always invited him to sing. At his home, he held song fests that drew a crowd of singers and musicians.

Significantly, Stanley maintained a close relationship with his niece Marie Blake, who was a talented musician herself. After moving from Moorestown to New York City, Marie studied piano with Carl Rossini Diton, the renowned pianist, composer, music director, and critic who was born in Philadelphia, Pennsylvania in 1886. Playing in the city's Greenwich Village most of her career, she became one of the area's leading jazz artists. Stanley, lacking a wife or children, bestowed Marie with his most valued possessions, the copyrights to his compositions and much of his memorabilia.

An inspiration to all who knew him, Stanley died in the Lakeland Sanitarium, in Atco, New Jersey, sometime in the 1960's. Before his death he asked of his family, friends, students, and peers: "Whatever you do, please don't let my music die." In honor of his memory, many of these individuals have joyously performed his hymns, for more than thirty years. Their actions are a testimony to his great influence and fine achievements.

BLAIR, ELLEN DIXON-HODGE (b. 1937), pianist, organist, choir director, accompanist. One of nine children born to George and Ellen (Alston) Dixon-Hodge, Ellen was born on May 11, 1937 in Camden, New Jersey. Her father was a native of New Jersey. Her mother, a street evangelist who was born in Littleton, North Carolina, moved to Camden as a baby. Educated in the public schools, Ellen graduated from Camden High School in 1956. She completed her postsecondary education at Camden County Vocational School, in

Pennsauken, earning an associates degree in licensed practical nursing in 1958. After finishing her training, Ellen obtained successive jobs as a licensed practical nurse (LPN) in several hospitals, and as a private duty registry nurse. Married to Edward Blair, Jr. December 27, 1958, they had one child, Deborah, born in 1959.

Singing hymns in church at an early age first inspired Ellen's great passion for music. This interest caused her to join the youth choir at her church, Mt. Olive Holy Temple in Philadelphia, Pennsylvania, at age ten. Whenever her choir performed for services, Ellen, who was enthralled by musicians, intently watched the organists who accompanied them.

As a little girl, Ellen also bought a harmonica, then taught herself to play it. Performing and singing, especially with her siblings and friends, was her favorite childhood pastime.

By the time she entered high school, Ellen decided that she would become a church musician. When James Marshall Wheeler, one of Camden's most prominent music teachers, became organist at Mt. Olive Holy Temple, she asked her father for piano lessons. However, she was unable to start her training until the next year, after moving to the home of her maternal grandmother, Annie Alston. Mastering the fundamentals, Ellen studied with Wheeler at his studio for three years. In order to practice at home, she bought her first piano, with earnings from a part-time job and the help of her grandmother's credit. Within a short time, Ellen joined her grandmother's church, Kaighn Avenue Baptist Church in Camden. Singing under the direction of Chris Payne, the church's very talented organist-choir director, helped foster her musical growth. Juanita Fernandez, another fine young organist who substituted for Payne while he briefly served in the military, was a second important role model.

After taking a short hiatus, Ellen resumed her musical pursuits in the early 1960's. She first expanded her skill through studies with Rodger Mario, a Camden resident whose teaching emphasis was European classical music. Subsequently, Ellen took advanced training under the tutelage of Kenny Cook, an accomplished musician from Lindenwold. During this period, he served as the organist at Nazarene

Baptist Church in Camden, then at Faith Holiness Tabernacle Church in Paulsboro. As a result of her intensive training, Ellen developed a varied repertoire of hymns, spirituals, gospel, and the classics. When under Cook's tutelage, she played in recitals at Faith Holiness and in the *Amateur Hour* at the Camden YWCA Through his recommendations, Ellen obtained her first professional work in the early 1970's. A concert appearance accompanying Linnie Lober, an exceptional soprano soloist, marked the official start of her career. Her initial position as an organist was at Friendship Baptist Church in Camden. Two years later, Ellen accepted a brief position at Allen AME Church in Williamstown.

Since 1980, Ellen has worked simultaneously at several southern New Jersey churches, often sharing appointments with her close musical associates, in particular Essie Holmes Voorhees and Audrey Canois Givens. She has served as the organist-choir director of Bethel AME Church in Paulsboro, at Mt. Olive Baptist Church in Haddonfield, and in positions at three Camden churches: the organist-choir director at the Broadway UM Church; the accompanist of the Male Chorus at New Mickle Baptist Church; the organist for the Chapel Choir of the Mount Olivet SDA Church. Between the late 1980's and 1990, Ellen studied music with Samuel Dockery, another prominent musician and teacher.

Currently residing in Camden, Ellen maintains her full schedule, playing for Bethel AME Church in Paulsboro, Flippen's Funeral Home in Camden, and as an accompanist for special programs. Each month, she also volunteers her time as the pianist for religious services at the Cooper River Nursing Home in Pennsauken, New Jersey. Gratified by her work, Ellen anticipates giving many more years of service to the church and her community.

BROWN, EMILY LUCKEN (1907–1986), pianist, organist, music teacher, choir director, accompanist, concert artist, radio broadcast performer. Emily was born on October 31, 1907 in Charleston, South Carolina. She was the youngest child of John and Emeline (Middleton) Lucken, who were both natives of Walterboro, South Carolina. Only three of the Lucken's seven children, born in Charleston between the years 1893 and 1907, survived at birth. They were, in order by age, all girls: Florence, Adrianna, and Emily.

Because of her father's gainful employment with the Standard Oil Company, Emily's family lived a comfortable, middle class life. For their grammar and high school education, she and her sisters attended a private school in Charleston, the Avery Institute, founded and operated by the American Missionary Association. Devoted church members, the family attended one of the city's churches, Zion Presbyterian Church, where her father served as a deacon.

In the Lucken household, playing the piano and singing together was their main form of entertainment. Since her mother firmly believed that one should read music, each daughter received private instruction. Very eager to learn after listening to her sisters' music lessons, Emily started playing the piano by ear at age five. As soon as her mother discovered her practice, she had Emily begin lessons immediately. Between the ages of five and eleven, Emily studied with several teachers, starting with her oldest sister, Florence. A talented pianist herself, Florence played for their church's Sunday school. Subsequently, Emily took lessons from a few music teachers in quick succession, followed by a longer period of study with Maud Smith Atkins, who greatly impressed her. While under Atkins' tutelage, she performed in her first public recital.

At the age of twelve, Emily began to play for Mt. Zion's Sunday school. By the time she completed grammar school, she was teaching music. Augmenting her skills by studying the pipe organ at age fifteen allowed her to become her church's organist within a year. During her tenure in this position, she performed in a number of concerts, presenting sacred and classical compositions.

Emily graduated from high school in 1925, then obtained work as a grammar school teacher in the rural districts of South Carolina. Traveling from her parents' home each day, she first taught at a school on St. John's Island, an island in Charleston Bay. Her next teaching position was in Monk's Corner.

In the late 1920's, Emily's cousin, Abel Generette, introduced her to Clarence Bowman Brown, whom she would later marry. A native of North Carolina, he was a restaurant maitre d' on the seasonal hotel circuit. Emily and Clarence were married in Hagerstown, Maryland, in April 1930. For a few months, they traveled and worked together. After becoming pregnant, Emily returned to South Carolina to give birth at her parents' home. The Browns had three children between the years 1931 and 1936: in order by age, they were named Clarence Jr., Ruth, and Sylvia. While their middle child was also born in Charleston, their youngest was born in Camden, New Jersey.

Emily and Clarence Sr. first moved to Camden after their son was born, renting an apartment in the downtown area. Following the birth of their daughter Ruth, her husband bought a barbershop as a business investment. Since there was an apartment above it, the family moved there. A short time later, Clarence Sr. opened a second enterprise, a saloon (he later owned and operated Brownie's Inn, in Batesville, a section of Delaware Township (Cherry Hill)). Meanwhile, besides raising her children, Emily continued her musical pursuits. In the mid 1930's, she served briefly as the organist of Macedonia AME Church in Camden. Prior to taking that position, Emily had started giving private music lessons in her home. Because of her expertise, she quickly obtained several students.

After her youngest daughter was born, Emily and her husband separated, and eventually divorced. Returning to South Carolina for a few years, she and her children lived alternately in Charleston and Walterboro, with her sisters and their families. To support her family, Emily took a position as a teacher in Russellville. By attending normal school during the summers, she obtained her teacher's certification in 1941.

Although her marriage had ended, Emily returned to Camden in 1942. Hired at RCA building electronic components, Emily became the first black woman employee to be promoted to the position of inspector. That same year, she and her children joined St. Augustine's Episcopal Church, located at 9th and Sycamore Streets in Camden. Converting from Presbyterianism, Emily was confirmed a member of the Episcopal Church in 1943.

As a substitute for James Marshall Wheeler, Emily became the organist at Kaighn Avenue Baptist Church in Camden. Wheeler, one of the city's eminent musicians and teachers, had taken a leave of absence to serve in the military. When he resumed his duties, Emily accepted positions at other churches, including Westville Baptist Church, and Baptist Temple Church, in Westville, New Jersey and Camden, respectively. Through her musical pursuits and her religious devotion, Emily spent virtually all day in church on Sundays. After attending early service at St. Augustine's, then playing for another church, she and her children went to evening programs, such as the Back Home Hour at Bethel AME Church in Camden. A convocation of people from all parts of the city, the proceedings featured congregational singing, along with lively entertainment by soloists and ensembles, including the popular Two Tones, Rose Henley and Beatrice Johnson.

In the mid 1940's, Emily left RCA and secured a position as a teacher at St. Bartholomew's Roman Catholic School, a Camden parochial school with grades kindergarten through twelfth. Employed there ten years, Emily taught the elementary classes. Besides teaching, she directed several of the high school students' musical productions. Combining her artistic interests and working with young people in this fashion greatly satisfied Emily. Because she dedicated her time to make school more interesting for the pupils, she was an especially beloved teacher.

When she first returned to the city, Emily resumed teaching piano and voice in her home. Quite successful in securing students, she presented them in annual recitals at churches, and other locations. In later years, Emily was quite pleased that several of her pupils became successful musicians, in particular Iona Davis Richardson, Herbert Nix, Jr., and Jeanne Heard Mosley.

For more than twenty years, Emily, who was prolific in her work and greatly admired for her versatility, accompanied many fine singers in concerts throughout the area. Two noteworthy individuals whom she played for were both Camden residents: Holton Hackett, and William Smith, one of her talented piano students. Hackett, a

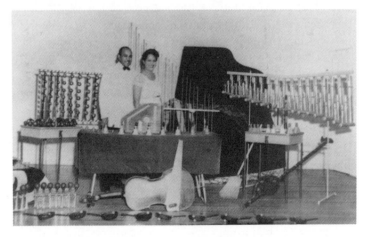

Above: The Kershaw Royal Singers, circa early 1950's. Recruited by Charles Kershaw (far right), Emily Lucken Brown accompanied the ensemble for twenty years, playing for their WKDN radio broadcasts in Camden, New Jersey, and U.S. tours. Below: After forming their duo, the Borden Bellringers, Brown's and Kershaw's popularity soared . This photo shows his amazing array of traditional and folk instruments. Courtesy of Ruth Brown Gantt.

baritone soloist, was best known for his work as a member of the Dra Mu Opera Company in Philadelphia, Pennsylvania. During the company's 1945-54 productions, he sang the lead roles of Valentin in *Faust*, Morales in *Carmen*, and Sylvio and Germont in *Pagliacci* [sic], as well as in the chorus. William Smith, established his professional singing career in Los Angeles, California in the 1960's. After performing with Pearl Bailey when she starred in the New York City Broadway production of *Hello Dolly*, he became her personal assistant.

In addition to working with individual artists, Emily formed a trio with two exceptional residents of Camden, coloratura soprano Gretchen Branche Waples, and flutist Louis Puggsley. Waples, a former student of two prominent New York voice coaches, Giuseppe Boghetti and Frank La Forge, had a brief career as a concert artist before her marriage to funeral director, Arthur Waples. Puggsley, a musician and conductor, belonged to more than one the black symphony orchestras that were active in New Jersey and Pennsylvania from the 1920's through the 1950's, most notably the Hunton Branch Symphony Orchestra of Camden, and the Philadelphia Concert Orchestra of Philadelphia. Advancing their mutual interests, Emily and her associates performed the classics, opera, and sacred music, throughout Camden, Woodbury, and other locales in southern New Jersey.

Sometime after 1950, Emily became the organist of her church, St. Augustine's. This gave her the opportunity to work with the Senior Choir and its director, S. Edward Davis, the founder of the celebrated Woodbury Choral Society. Because of her commitment playing on a radio broadcast early Sunday morning, Emily played exclusively for the 11:00 service. Assistant organists, including Juanita Fernandez, provided music at the 7:30 A.M. service.

From the early 1950's, Emily was best known for her work with Charles V. Kershaw, who was a resident of Bordentown, New Jersey, on the religious program entitled the *Kershaw Hour*. Broadcast live every Saturday and Sunday morning at 7:00 A.M., it was aired on station WKDN (later WTMR) in Camden. Kershaw, who served as the producer and director, secured Emily's services as the program's pianist when founding the show. The *Kershaw Hour* featured the

Kershaw Royal Singers, an ensemble comprised of vocalists from Camden and smaller towns. Ranging in size from twelve to twenty-five members, they performed all types of sacred music. A phenomenal success, the Kershaw Royal Singers toured extensively throughout the United States. While the group's income covered travel expenses, it was not enough to pay salaries. Despite the lack of compensation, many dedicated individuals joined the Kershaw Royal Singers through the years. They included these talents: Susie LaMar Morris Parker, N. Henry Ingram, Sr., Sam Mitchell, Martha Thompson, Julius Jackson, James Jackson, Vera Jackson, Donald "Duckey" Birts, Matthew Hickson, and Glynne Alveria Davis. The Kershaw Royal Singers also hosted guest performers, such as Chester and Ruth Worthington, Sr., a noted husband and wife duo from Berlin, New Jersey.

As an off-shoot of their work on the *Kershaw Hour*, Emily and Charles Kershaw, who was a consummate entertainer, formed a duo called the Borden Bellringers. Active in the 1950's and 1960's, the act consisted of Emily on keyboard, and Kershaw playing an assortment of instruments. His fantastic collection included; hand bells of every size; sleigh bells; chimes; horns; a violoncello; a saw; spoons; and other assorted percussive implements. Booking appearances through an agent, they toured extensively performing in schools, churches, community halls, and theaters. A profitable act that elevated Emily and Kershaw to celebrity status, their more elaborate productions featured his magic show. At times, Susie LaMar Morris Parker and other associates joined them in performance.

Because of his deteriorating health, Kershaw retired from the *Kershaw Hour* in 1970. Upon his departure, one of its most dedicated members, N. Henry Ingram, Sr., became producer, securing the program license renewal from the Federal Communications Commission under a new name, *Words and Music*. After assisting Ingram for a short time, Emily left the show herself. Her departure was the start of her semi-retirement.

Working sporadically from the early 1970's until 1983, Emily substituted for vacationing organists or accepted temporary positions until a church found a full time musician. The First Church Christ

Scientist and St. Andrews Episcopal, both in Camden, were two churches that she assisted in this manner. She helped produce the *Amateur Hour*, a competition for local talent, held at the Stevens Street YWCA in Camden under the direction of Henrietta Fuller Robinson, a dynamic musician and music teacher. In the mid 1970's, Emily joined Camp Farthest Out (CFO), a religious association, at St. Stephen's Episcopal Church in Philadelphia. While attending CFO retreats, she occasionally served as the musical director. Retiring completely in 1983 because of her declining health, Emily spent her final years living alternately with her daughters; the summer months in New Jersey with Ruth, and the remainder of the year in Florida with Sylvia.

Because of her deep religious devotion, Emily only accepted a limited number of awards for her more than fifty years of service as a musician. Believing she was blessed to have received her musical training and experience, she professed: "I am happy to share my gifts with other people." Two awards that Emily was honored to receive were the Chapel of Four Chaplains Award and a citation from the Marian Anderson Music Guild, Camden branch of NANM, whose programs she attended. She was the composer of one unpublished hymn, *No One Can Help You But The Lord*. Having made an exceptional contribution to the church and to her community, Emily died on November 21, 1986 at West Jersey Hospital, in Voorhees, New Jersey.

COLLINS, ISABELLE M. (b. 1902), vocalist, pianist, organist, concert artist, music teacher, vocal coach. The only child of Raleigh and Lucy Ann (Dickerson) Crews, Isabelle was born in Edgewood, Pennsylvania on January 8, 1902. Her mother and father were natives of Virginia.

A short time after Isabelle was born, her family moved to a farm on the outskirts of Pennington, a township in Burlington County, New Jersey. Initially, her father worked the land to support their family. Since he was unable to earn sufficient income as a farmer, they moved into the town, where he obtained a more lucrative job. To augment the family's income, her mother earned money doing housework. Because of their religious convictions, the Crews family attended the First Baptist Church in Pennington, at Crawley and Academy Streets.

Educated in Burlington County public and private schools, Isabelle entered grammar school in Pennington at age six. After graduating from eighth grade, she attended the high school in Hopewell. A year later, Isabelle transferred into the academic course at the New Jersey Manual Training and Industrial School for Colored Youth, a well-known private institution located in Bordentown.

By the time she was school age, Isabelle developed a considerable interest in music, fostered by singing hymns and Negro spirituals in Sunday School. Her parents, intent on giving her the best education within their financial means, provided her with piano lessons at age eight. During her study of the basics, Isabelle displayed ample talent. At age twelve, an even greater indication of her musical potential was evident as she sang in her church's choir. The beauty of Isabelle's voice brought her to the attention of Lester Bingley, an expert musician who lived in Trenton, New Jersey. Impressed by her tonal quality, Bingley gave Isabelle her first private voice lessons at age sixteen. His training and encouragement, combined with her music studies at the Bordentown school, was a key influence in her decision to become a professional musician.

After graduating from high school, Isabelle moved to a cousin's home in Philadelphia and entered Temple University, as a violin major, in 1919. Upon her withdrawal from school at the close of her freshman year, she continued her music studies through private lessons in piano and voice. Between 1920 and 1930, Isabelle trained with teachers who were among the elite of the concert world, most notably the great contralto, Marian Anderson. After six years of training that ended when Anderson went abroad, Isabelle studied with Giuseppe Boghetti, Anderson's vocal coach. Simultaneous to her vocal training, Isabelle studied piano with Carl Rossini Diton (1886–1962), another great influence in her life, at his studio in Philadelphia. A native of the city, Diton was an accomplished musician, composer, and former college professor, who had studied music theory in Munich, Germany in 1910. When Isabelle launched her concert career, he became her first manager and coached her for performances. Since he was a charter member (and later fourth president) of the National Association of Negro Musicians, the historic organization founded in Chicago in 1919 by the upper echelon of black artists, Diton encouraged Isabelle to join. Following his recommendation, she became a member in 1921. Isabelle also studied piano with another fine teacher, W. Russell Johnson, the founder of the Philadelphia chapter of NANM, that bore his name in later years.

While engaged in her studies, Isabelle, who by then had rented an apartment, pursued her profession, initially by teaching piano and voice. In 1924, she became the assistant organist at her church, Bethel Baptist Church, on Powelton Avenue near her residence. After attaining great expertise as a lyric soprano, Isabelle established herself as a concert artist in the early 1930's. She performed admirably in English, French, German, Italian, and Spanish, favoring the works of Mendelssohn, Rachmaninoff, Beethoven, Mozart, Hadyn, Handel, Debussy, Fauré, and Strauss. Her extensive repertoire included the works of contemporary black composers, notably R. Nathaniel Dett, Harry T. Burleigh, Hall Johnson, Diton, Florence Price, and William Dawson. Guided by a succession of personal managers after Diton moved to New York City, Isabelle secured a number of advantageous appearances from her career's outset.

In 1935, Isabelle married Reverend Douglass Collins, a widower with five children, at the Galilee ME Church in Englewood, New Jersey. A native of Boydton, Virginia and raised in Brooklyn, New York, he was a lawyer and a minister, having earned a degree in law (L.L.B.) from Suffolk Law School in Boston, Massachusetts, and a degree in theology (S.T.B.) from Lincoln University in Oxford, Pennsylvania. Isabelle's step-children were Mable, Evelyn, Douglass, Ruth, and William.

Presented with the opportunity to devote her appreciable talents to her faith, Isabelle served as the organist-choir director, or choir director, of eight, of the nine churches her husband pastored. A member of the Delaware Conference of the Methodist Episcopal (Methodist after 1939) Church from 1935 until 1961, his assignments, listed in sequential order, were to these parishes: Galilee ME Church in Englewood; the church of Deal Island, Maryland; the church of New Castle, Delaware; the church of Elkton, Maryland; Clair Memorial Church, Jersey City, New Jersey; St. John's Methodist Church,

ISABELLE COLLINS

SOPRANO

TIMES HALL

240 West 44th Street New York

SUNDAY EVE.   MAY 1st at 8:30

PROGRAM OVERLEAF

A refined lyric soprano, Collins's spring 1949 appearance at New York City's Times Hall propelled her into the national spotlight, and a tour, starting in 1950, of the United States, Canada, the Caribbean, and Europe. The evening was also memorable for her premiere of "Little Things," an art song by Florence Price, the noted black composer.

Orange, New Jersey; St. Matthew's Methodist Church, Ossining, New York; Whatcoat Methodist Church, Dover, Delaware; Ferry Avenue Methodist Church, Camden, New Jersey. Additionally, Isabelle was elected president of the following three organizations: the Northern End of the Philadelphia District of the Delaware Conference of Minister's Wives; the National Association of Minister's Wives of Camden and Vicinity (1947–1953); the Women's Society of Christian Service.

Despite her demanding schedule, Isabelle, tirelessly proceeded with her concert career. She was assisted in this pursuit by her husband, who served as her legal advisor. Reaching the pinnacle of her success, Isabelle secured an appearance at Times Hall, in New York City on May 1, 1949. Her visible nervousness did not detract from her overall performance, and favorable reviews in the *New York Times*, the *Amsterdam News*, and other local press broadened her appeal:

> Isabelle Collins, soprano, gave a recital in Times Hall last night. She sang with accuracy and delicacy.
>
> In her featured number, 'Hear Ye, Israel', from Mendelssohn's 'Elijah', she developed considerable intensity, particularly in her vibrant register, notwithstanding there was a persistent tremolo in her voice.
>
> *—New York Times,* May 2, 1949
>
> Isabelle Collins gave a concert in Times Hall on Sunday evening, May 1. Her well chosen program included classics, some lieder, a Mendelssohn aria from 'Elijah', art songs and Negro spirituals by Dett and Johnson.
>
> WE heard the first group and were immediately impressed by the singer's excellent tone production. She has excellent stage composure as well as definite musicianship. Marc D'Albert gave able assistance at the piano.
>
> *—Amsterdam News,* May 7, 1949

Her appearance was also noteworthy for the first New York performance of *Little Things,* an art song composed by Florence Price, and the first public performance of Hall Johnson's arrangement of the spiritual, *They Led My Lord Away.* Capitalizing upon this publicity the next year, Isabelle started touring extensively, in the United States, Canada, the Caribbean, and Europe.

With an unwavering commitment that exceeded forty years, Isabelle also promoted NANM's mission of encouraging the development of black musicians nationwide, by assuming various committee appointments and elected posts within the organization. In 1940 she became a branch organizer. In that capacity, she was the sole founder of three chapters: Collins-Berksteiner Chapter, in Ossining, New York; W. C. Handy Chapter, in Dover, Delaware; Trenton Chapter, in Trenton, New Jersey. Reverend J. Ferman Little, the pastor of the First Church of God in Camden, and Isabelle also co-founded the Camden Chapter (renamed the Marian Anderson Music Guild) in 1971. For several years, she and her husband enthusiastically hosted NANM concerts and meetings at their churches, resulting in awards for outstanding service for each of them. Within this period, Isabelle served in these local, regional, and national offices: first assistant director of the Eastern Region, president of the Collins-Berksteiner Chapter, president of the W. C. Handy Chapter, and ten years on the national board of directors.

In 1961, just two months after becoming pastor of the Ferry Avenue Methodist Church, Isabelle's husband died suddenly. At the request of the Delaware Conference, she remained in Camden to serve as the organist-choir director of the Parkside Methodist (UM, after 1968) Church for five years. Having deciding to become a permanent resident of the city when she retired from this position, she retained her membership in the church. Besides singing as a soloist with Parkside UM's Senior Choir, she later directed its Golden Age Choir.

From the mid 1960's through the early 1980's, Isabelle maintained a full schedule. She taught from a studio in her home on Park Boulevard, appeared in concerts, and helped develop the activities of the Camden chapter of NANM. For many years, Isabelle belonged to the South Jersey Music Teachers Association, as well as a civic association, the NAACP. Highly esteemed for her fine performances, precise conducting, and able teaching, she was awarded numerous citations for her exceptional achievements and dedication.

Although she decreased her activities during the mid 1980's, Isabelle never fully retired from her pursuits, musical and otherwise. Still vital at age of ninety-one, she traveled to western Africa. In her apartment at the Riverview Towers in Camden, she continued teaching until 1994. Now, Isabelle periodically directs and performs in programs at her residence and at her church.

DAVIS, S[AMUEL] EDWARD (1905–1993), pianist, organist, choral director, chorister, educator. Born 1905 in Crumpton, Maryland, Edward, as he preferred to be called, was third of the eight children of Reverend Joseph L. and Mary Elizabeth (Ward) Davis. A Methodist minister, Edward's father was born in Maryland on June 6, 1864. After completing his early education, he had earned a degree in theology from the Princess Anne Academy in Baltimore, Maryland. During his ministry, he served churches in three states: Maryland, Pennsylvania, and New Jersey. Likewise a Maryland native, Edward's mother was born April 15, 1877. Her education included training in music. Naturally gifted, she played the piano and was an accomplished singer. Edward's parents, who married on June 21, 1899, met as members of the same church; his father was its pastor, his mother a soloist on the choir. A widower at that time, Edward's father also had four children, Leroy, Norwood, Martie, and Viola, from his first wife, Helene. The younger set of Davis children, born between 1900 and 1920, were, in order by age, William, Mary, S. Edward, George, Beatrice, Dorothy, Earl, and Barbara.

When he was two or three years old, Edward's family moved to Philadelphia, Pennsylvania. They resided in the city for nearly fourteen years. During that period, he, along with his brothers and sisters, attended the city's public schools.

By virtue of having a minister as their father and a musician as their mother, Edward and his siblings were taught religious music from birth. As part of their private family worship, they sang grace at meals. Although his mother trained them to play the piano, Edward, showing a great propensity for music, required very little instruction. Instead, after listening to his older sister lessons, he started playing by ear, at age five or six. He remained essentially self-taught throughout his early childhood. Since he became quite proficient,

Edward's father hired him as their church's organist-choir director at age twelve. Despite his youth, he was self-assured and ably served in this position for several years. Edward used his earnings to pay for private music instruction.

After graduating from grammar school, Edward enrolled in Central High School, an elite, all-boys school. Within a year or two, because his father was assigned to a church in Woodbury, New Jersey, he transferred to the Woodbury High School. Upon his enrollment, Edward, instilled with great racial pride by his parents, successfully challenged the school's practice of seating black students in the back of the classroom. Subsequently, he and his classmates were seated alphabetically, by last name, without regard to race. A busy participant in extra-curricular activities, Edward, a high tenor until his voice deepened to second bass, sang in the Glee Club. As a track star, he won numerous meets and regional acclaim as an athlete.

When he finished high school, Edward went to work for the Socony Vacuum Oil Company in Paulsboro, a town close to Woodbury, in the mid to late 1920's. Meanwhile, he continued serving as organist at his father's church. Although life was harsh with the Depression's onset, Edward decided to attend college to earn a degree in music. In 1932, he entered Temple University, in Philadelphia, studying harmony and composition. However, due to the lack of financial support, Edward withdrew after one semester. This bitter disappointment was a key factor that, before long, motivated him to his greatest achievements as a musician.

At the start of the 1930's, prompted by his father's transfer to a church in another city, Edward had secured a position as the organist-choir director of Bethel AME Church, on Carpenter Street in Woodbury. During his tenure, he entered the church's Young People's Choir in a statewide competition, founded in 1924 by the New Jersey Manual Training and Industrial School for Colored Youth in Bordentown, New Jersey. The annual event was part of the school's Decoration Day (Memorial Day) observances for its students, faculty, family members, and the public. Consistently attracting at least eight entrants, all were required to perform the same selection. Bethel AME's Young People's Choir, highly successful under Edward's direction, won first place in three consecutive contests. This allowed them to retain permanent possession of the trophy cup awarded those years. Often, nationally prominent musicians were judges; Harry T. Burleigh, the renowned black baritone and composer, was one.

In the mid 1930's, Edward met Theresa M. Smith. A resident of Cape May Court House, New Jersey, she taught elementary school in Jericho Township, a small rural town in Salem County, New Jersey. The couple were married in 1936. Within a short time, they had three children: twins Sylvia and Warren, and Rodney.

The same year he married, because of his realization that many black children were in the same predicament that led him to quit Temple University, Edward resolved to help needy students pursue their college education. To accomplish his goal, while simultaneously promoting a cultural activity in the black community, he founded the Woodbury Choral Society, in October of 1936.

Holding auditions, Edward selected sixteen members, residents of southern New Jersey, Philadelphia, and Centreville, Maryland. His Bethel AME Church choir comprised the core group of singers. After electing officers and a directors board, Edward and the members dedicated themselves to financing a scholarship fund, by presenting an annual concert and offering associate memberships to the general public. Under his direction for twenty-six years, the society's active members (performers) eventually exceeded forty. Although the majority were black, a fact frequently mentioned in press reviews was the chorus's inter-racial composition. Among the founding members were Charles W. Brown, assistant conductor, Sarah C. Williams, accompanist, and Corinne Pope, accompanist. Dedicated members who served in key positions at a later time, such as Nellie Lambourne Kehlet, assistant director, and Clara Brazier, accompanist, also contributed to the ensemble's lasting success.

Initially meeting at Bethel AME Church, Edward rehearsed the group weekly. He was a very disciplined conductor, always starting on time, and demanding the same of his members. Eventually overcoming opposition from the local school board, Edward secured use of the Woodbury High School for rehearsals, and a concert the following spring. Appearing before a capacity crowd, the Woodbury

Entrants in the statewide choir competition held by the New Jersey Manual Training and Industrial School for Colored Youth in Bordentown, Edward Davis and the Young People's Choir of Woodbury's Bethel AME Church earned a trophy cup for their three consecutive wins in the early 1930's. Foreground: Reverend Thomas. Front row, left to right: Helen Harrison, Genevieve Brown, Theresa Smith, Dorothy Davis, Mary Davis, Beatrice Davis, Marguerite Gould, Helen Johns Fisher. Back row, left to right: Thomas Waples, Amos Galloway, Walter Gordon, Arthur Browne, Mercer Allen, Claude Kennard, Sylvanus Browne, S. Edward Davis, organist-choir director. Courtesy Elmira Howard Davis.

Directed by S. Edward Davis (standing center front) for twenty-six years, the Woodbury Choral Society charmed audiences with a marvelous presentation of sacred and secular choral music. Photo, taken at the Woodbury High School circa mid 1950's, courtesy of Elmira Howard Davis.

Choral Society premiered May 28, 1937. The ensemble, with its Male Quartette and Female Chorus, delighted the appreciative audience with their theme song, E. J. Stenson's *Prayer Perfect,* and a liberal selection of hymns, spirituals, classics, and secular choral music.

Establishing their tradition of featuring prominent or up-and-coming musicians from the area, Edward and the choir hosted two guest artists that evening, Edna M. Casper, lyric soprano, and Ruth Calloway Bounds, pianist. In the ensuing years, these artists were among the invited performers: Leon B. Wisdom, violinist (and alumni of the Curtis Institute of Philadelphia); James H. Burch, tenor; Ruth L. Morris, soprano; G. Garner Waples, vocalist; Joseph H. Lockwood, pianist; Holton Hackett, baritone; Roland Wiggins, pianist (and future jazz musician and educator); the Woodbury String Trio; Eutha Davis, soprano; Nellie Lambourne Kehlet, contralto; Elaine Washington, lyric soprano; the Woodbury Symphony Orchestra, under the direction of Guido Terranova; Hidetaro Suzuki, violinist.

By the early 1940's, the Woodbury Choral Society received critical acclaim, largely due to Edward's musical expertise and leadership. Their spring concert, held annually except for four years during World War II, was a major social event, attracting a diverse audience of black professionals, wealthy white patrons, and music lovers of all classes, from the Delaware Valley (southern New Jersey, southeastern Pennsylvania, and Delaware), and Maryland. This feat soon brought them invitations, that they gladly accepted, to perform in other cities in southern New Jersey and Maryland. By 1950, Edward and the society had presented three students with four hundred dollar scholarships. At the height of their success between 1950 and the early 1960's, they made eighteen additional awards. Their popularity in that period was also evident as the associate members, whose names were listed in their annual program booklet, increased to nearly nine hundred. Edward retired as the director in 1963. Although never matching these same deeds after his departure, the organization continued in existence through the late 1970's.

While pursuing his calling, Edward sustained two tragic losses, the death of his wife, followed by the death of his son, Warren. After his period of mourning, Edward married Elmira Howard, a resident of Camden, New Jersey, a school teacher and organist-choir director at Ferry Avenue Methodist Church in Camden, on February 22, 1947. An important influence in his life, she convinced him to return to college. Edward, arranging to work nights at the Socony Vacuum Oil Company, enrolled at Glassboro State College (later Rowan College), in Glassboro, New Jersey. Graduating with his bachelor of science degree in 1950, he later entered graduate school at Temple University, receiving a master of science, then a master of arts degree. After completing his studies, he obtained positions as a teacher, vice-principal, and as the first African American principal of Salem High School, in Salem, New Jersey. The latter position he held from 1969 until his June 1978 retirement.

Through the years, Edward engaged in several other musical pursuits. A member of St. Augustine's Episcopal Church in Camden, he served as its organist-choir director for more than twenty years. He also sang second bass in the Singing City Choir of Philadelphia, under the directorship of Dr. Elaine Brown. Constantly developing his craft, Edward studied organ with renowned Camden musician, James Marshall Wheeler, and choral conducting with Brown.

Dedicated to life-long community service, Edward, notably, was the first African American Field Commissioner of the Gloucester County Boy Scout Organization, establishing troops in the southern New Jersey communities of Jericho, Pennsgrove, Glassboro, North Woodbury, and South Woodbury. Working with two other non-profit organizations, he was a trustee of the United Fund of Gloucester County, and the music chairperson of the local Good Will Council. Additionally, Edward was the first, and as of the mid 1990's, only African American to serve as president of the Woodbury Rotary Club.

After residing in Woodbury for twenty-five years, Edward and Elmira moved to West Deptford, New Jersey. Throughout his career, he was highly esteemed for his excellence and his devotion. On January 1, 1993, Edward died at the age of eighty-seven. His personal collection of memorabilia, maintained by his widow, consists of valuable reel-to-reel tapes of the Woodbury Choral Society's concerts, along with correspondence, program booklets, plaques, and photographs. A brief sketch of his life is published in Dr. Rebecca Batts Butler's *Portraits of Black Role Models in the History of Southern New Jersey*, Acme Craftsmen Publishers, 1985.

DURHAM, ALICE BAUGHN [DAVIS] (b. 1928), pianist, organist, choir director, accompanist, arranger, music teacher. The eldest of Elijah and Gertie Beatrice (Turner) Baughn's two children, Alice was born on May 3, 1928, in Philadelphia, Pennsylvania. Her brother, Elijah Jr., was born in 1930.

A native of Crouch, Virginia, Alice's father, who had an eighth grade education, was employed as a bellhop at the Strath Haven Inn, in Swarthmore, Pennsylvania. Working at the exclusive hotel, patronized by a wealthy clientele, provided him with a lucrative salary and generous tips. A high school graduate, Alice's mother, who was a native of eastern Texas, came to Philadelphia to attend a technical school. A short time after her parents met, they were married and settled into a home in Philadelphia. At that time, her mother ended her educational pursuits and became a house wife. A year after Alice was born, her family moved into a home in Morton, Pennsylvania.

In 1931, Alice's father, accepting an opportunity offered to him through his employment, bought a three story house in Swarthmore. When they moved into their new home, in a neighborhood consisting of four blocks of "colored" families, Alice was three and her brother one. To earn additional income for the upkeep of the house, her parents rented rooms on the third floor to four boarders, co-workers of her father. Belonging to the Episcopal denomination, her family attended St. Mary's Episcopal Church in Chester, Pennsylvania.

Within that year, a severe burn to Alice's hand was the unlikely impetus that effected her early study of music. Although she was only three, the doctor who examined her recommended that she take piano lessons as therapy for the injury. Within a short time, Alice started taking instruction every two weeks from Mrs. Walker, a music teacher who lived in the town. As her therapy corrected the damage to her hand, Alice progressed quickly, showing a great aptitude for music that she inherited from her father, who played by ear. At age five, through Mrs. Walkers suggestion, Alice started weekly lessons with a more proficient teacher, Amelia Goodman, who resided in Chester.

Educated in the Swarthmore public schools, Alice entered kindergarten at age five. Having the opportunity to participate in the school's Christmas program, she amazed the teachers by playing *O Tannenbaum*. From first through fourth grade, Alice, along with the other black children, studied in a segregated classroom, the Union Room. For the remainder of their schooling, she and her classmates were in integrated classes.Continuing to study piano and rudimentary theory under Miss Goodman, Alice, who was thoughtful, and reserved by nature, performed in annual recitals that soon established her reputation as a very capable musician. At age eleven, she became the organist and choir director of Wesley AME Church in Swarthmore, gaining valuable experience. When Alice was sixteen, Miss Goodman advised her to seek a more knowledgeable teacher for advanced training. Enrolling in the Philadelphia Musical Academy as a student of piano, she came under the tutelage of Helene Diedrichs. Through the encouragement of her high school music teacher, who also recognized her extraordinary talent that included perfect pitch, Alice then decided to major in music in college.

In the fall of 1946 following her June graduation from high school, Alice, who was the recipient of Swarthmore High School's senior class scholarship, entered Fisk University, in Nashville, Tennessee, to pursue her degree. The following year, because of deteriorating health, she transferred to the Philadelphia Musical Academy and resumed study with Diedrichs. Until her senior year, Alice aspired to a career on the concert stage. However, despite being confident in her expertise, she agreed with her teacher's assessment that her prospects were limited as a black musician.

Instead of graduating from the Academy, Alice married George Davis, a native of Donora, Pennsylvania, in 1950. He was a graduate of Cheyney Teachers College, an historic black college in Cheyney, Pennsylvania. Founded 1837 on a farm near Philadelphia, the school was closed, then re-opened in 1852 as the Institute for Colored Youth, on Lombard Street in the city of Philadelphia. A teacher by profession, George worked for the school district of Philadelphia. Alice and George settled into an apartment in the city on Dearborn Street. In due time, the couple had three sons: Warren, Wayne, and Ward.

When first married, Alice worked as an accompanist at the Judimar School of Dance in Philadelphia. Operated by Marion Durham Cuyjet, a nationally prominent African American dancer and teacher, it was the city's premier training ground in classical ballet, modern, primitive, and interpretive dance for black artists. At that time, among its students who became extraordinary stars of the dance stage, were Judith Jamison and Gaston DeVigne, Jr. During Alice's six year tenure at Judimar, she played in the studio and in the annual productions. In the 1951 Town Hall performance, entitled *Chopiniana*, Alice, especially featured by Cuyjet, exhibited her distinctive command of her craft. Cuyjet also recorded Alice's performance of Chopin, and sold copies to the parents of her students.

After living in Philadelphia for four years, Alice and her husband built a rancher and moved to Berlin. Because she was in her second pregnancy and the commute was difficult, she resigned from her position at Judimar in 1956. Resuming her musical pursuits in 1957 after giving birth, Alice became the pianist-choir director at Greengrove Baptist Church in Berlin and Calvary Baptist Church, located in West Atco, in succession. During the early 1960's, she accompanied Lavinia N. Franklin, a noted contralto from Washington D.C., in three memorable performances at Glassboro State College (later Rowan College), in Glassboro, New Jersey, and in the District of Columbia. Recruited by the owner of a music school, Alice increased her income by teaching accordion, piano, guitar, and organ at two Roman Catholic schools, St. Lawrence, in Berlin, and Mt. Carmel, in Lindenwold. Between 1964 and 1966, she also served as the organist of the Good Shepherd Church, an Episcopal church in Berlin. At the same time, she founded and directed the South Jersey Fellowship Choir, an inter-racial group of twenty-five to thirty-five singers from Berlin, Atco, Chesilhurst, Sicklerville, and Camden. Rehearsing weekly, they gave an elaborate concert each year, performing four classical compositions, four Negro spirituals, and four contemporary works.

64

Divorced in 1963, Alice married Joseph Durham three years later. Prior to the birth of their son Whitney, she stopped teaching at the Catholic schools and directing her choral ensemble.

In 1967, Alice resumed teaching by offering private music instruction in her home, comprised of a thorough training in the classics. As a result of her expertise, she secured numerous students, some of whom pursued successful professional careers as musicians, such as Debra Stroud and Trina McIntosh. Through personal referrals, Alice also obtained engagements performing at fundraisers, cocktail parties, birthday parties, weddings, and other special functions throughout southern New Jersey. With a repertoire that ranged from Bach and Bartok to Debussy and Gershwin, she was much sought after as an accompanist and played frequently for vocalists in concert. Likewise offering her services as an arranger, Alice transcribed and harmonized songs for local composers who did not read music.

Within this same period, her employment as a Head Start teacher motivated Alice to continue her education. Specializing in early childhood development, she earned an associate degree in 1974, a bachelor of science degree in 1975, and a master of social work degree in 1981 from Camden County College, in Blackwood, New Jersey, Glassboro State College, and Rutger's University, in Camden, respectively. Certified by Delaware and New Jersey, Alice subsequently obtained these positions: Education Coordinator for Head Start, Camden County, the director of St. Michael's Nursery in Wilmington, Delaware, and Contract Coordinator, with the Division of Youth and Family Services, for the State of New Jersey. Always concerned with the quality of the music programs at the various facilities under her charge, she reserved time to train the teachers in order to upgrade the curriculum.

Held in high esteem in the community, Alice, who has engaged in teaching and performing for over thirty-five years, remains devoted to her work. Although deeply satisfied by each of her life-long pursuits, she has affirmed: "I derive the greatest personal sense of reward from teaching music." A brief sketch of Alice's life is published in Dr. Rebecca Batts Butler's *Portraits of Black Role Models in the History of Southern New Jersey*, Acme Craftsmen Publishers, 1985.

EVERS, MAXINE MONROE (b. 1930), vocalist, choir director, pianist, music teacher. Born in Holly Grove, Arkansas on January 27, 1930, Maxine was the only child of Willie and Naomi (Brister) Monroe. Her father, born near Holly Grove on November 8, 1911, was the youngest of three children born to Sanders and Gussie (Cowan) Monroe. His parents had traveled to Arkansas from Georgia, via covered wagon, in the late 1880's. Maxine's mother, born near Nolan, Arkansas, was the fifth of the seven children of Reverend and Mrs. William Henry Brister. A talented vocalist, she, along with members of her family, sang in local churches, schools, and lodges. Married in 1928, Maxine's parents were sharecroppers, raising cotton. Both were devout members of the AME church, and strict adherents of church doctrine. Educated in a one room church school, they received very little formal education.

For the first seven years of her life, Maxine's family lived in a home that had been a school for "colored" children. Educated in the county's public schools, she attend a segregated school located in a small town four miles away. Working on the farm as a small child, Maxine's chores included carrying coal and water to the field workers. She especially enjoyed watching the animals, visiting her maternal grandparents, and most of all, attending the local AME church on Sundays. When Maxine was nine, she and her parents moved to Philadelphia, Pennsylvania, where she completed her grammar and secondary education. After settling in the city, they joined Mother Bethel AME Church, the nation's first AME church. (Organized July 29, 1794 by Richard Allen, its first pastor and the first bishop of the denomination, the church arose from the Free African Society established in 1787 by Allen and Absalom Jones. The latter, first ordained a Methodist minister, then Episcopal priest, founded the African Episcopal Church of St. Thomas, the nation's oldest black Episcopal church, dedicated July 17, 1794.) Subsequent to attending Mother Bethel, the Monroe family joined Morris Brown AME Church, also in Philadelphia.

Through her mother's influence, Maxine developed an interest in music before she was school age. After learning to sing hymns and spirituals as a small child, she received her first music lessons in Philadelphia, from Myrtle Van Buren Watson, at age ten. A stellar pianist, church musician, and teacher, she had trained at the Yale Conservatory of Music as a child, and later at Temple University's School of Music. Watson instructed Maxine in piano and voice, who delighted by her lessons, studied classical, opera, light opera, and sacred music. Provided with a solid foundation, she next studied with William Burton, at his studio in the city, and with Professor Harry Grier, at the Theodore Presser School of Music, a respected institution in the city.

Already displaying ample talent while under Van Buren's tutelage, Maxine was given many opportunities to perform. By the age of twelve, she joined her church's junior choir and became a regular vocalist on the local radio program, *Paresian Taylor's Amateur Hour.* Performing popular show music and jazz tunes on live broadcasts broadened her range of musical experience. As a teenager, she was a member of the Junior Chorus of the renowned Dra Mu Opera Company, the African American ensemble founded in 1945 by Raymond Lowden Smith, a noted musician and conductor of the all-black Philadelphia Concert Orchestra (formerly E. Gilbert Anderson Memorial Symphony Orchestra).

In 1949, after graduating from high school, Maxine married Ulysses Evers in Clarendon, Arkansas. Self-employed, he owned a dry cleaning and laundry business. Besides working with her husband, Maxine studied a liberal arts curriculum at Arkansas State Teachers College. From their union, five children were born: Ulysses Jr., Morgan J., Naomi, Phyllis, and Marshall.

A deep religious conviction and a desire to please her parents inspired Maxine to work in the ministry of music within the church. In her first position that lasted nearly sixteen years, she was the director of the music program for the Youth Department and Sunday school of the First Baptist MB Church in Holly Grove. Whenever she visited her parents, who had moved to Atco, New Jersey during her final year of high school, Maxine also assisted Grant AME Church, in the neighboring town of Chesilhurst, with its music program.

In 1966, Maxine and her family moved to Atco, near her parents. Continuing her musical pursuits, she became the full-time choir director of Grant AME Church. Under her direction twenty-eight years, its Senior Choir traveled extensively, performing throughout the state, in New York, and in North Carolina. Maxine, incorporating teaching into her work, held classes for her choir members and the youth of the church. Because of her successful efforts, Grant AME later bestowed her with the title, minister of music.

In the 1970's, Maxine furthered her education, studying music and other subjects, at three New Jersey institutions: piano at the Haddonfield Conservatory of Music, in Haddonfield; church music at Drew University, in Madison; liberal arts at Camden County College, in Blackwood. During this time, in addition to her work at Grant AME, she played for the Greater Calvary Baptist Church in West Atco, and the Seventh-day Adventist Church in Newtonville. Occasionally appearing in individual concerts, she performed at Mt. Hope UAME Church in Camden, and the Seventh-day Adventist churches in Newtonville and the city of Glassboro.

Regarding the work of a church musician as a great responsibility, Maxine, throughout the years, maintained: "the musician, next to the preacher, is the most important part of the church." In judgement of her career, she stated: "Being involved in music has been a bittersweet experience for me. There have been sacrifices and many rewards. The years of study, training, and training others have been a humbling experience. I have grown spiritually and found that many of the things I believed were important in the past are no longer important." Inspired by her deep conviction and great sense of accomplishment, she has served both church and community with distinction. Semi-retired since 1994, Maxine presently plays for Grant AME on alternate Sundays.

FERNANDEZ [FERNANDERS], JUANITA ALVERA (1930–1995), pianist, organist, music teacher, vocalist. Juanita, who was the eldest of three children, was born to Benjamin Sadler and Mattie (Gardenhire) Fernanders on May 8, 1930 in Camden, New Jersey. Her father, also born in Camden, was a federal government employee. A native of Clarksville, South Carolina, her mother worked at the Campbell Soup Company. Juanita's siblings were Clarence W. and Charles E. Fernanders. Notably, her paternal grandfather, Benjamin M. Fernanders, was a bishop in the Union African Methodist Episcopal denomination. Her family worshipped at Chestnut Street UAME Church in Camden. Eventually, Juanita adopted an alternate spelling of her surname, changing it to Fernandez.

Educated in the public schools, Juanita attended the John Greenleaf Whittier Grammar School, Cooper B. Hatch Junior High School, and Camden High School, graduating from the latter's academic course in 1948. In the fall of that same year, she entered Glassboro State College (later Rowan College), studying piano, organ, and music education. Upon completing her degree in 1952, Juanita obtained a position as a teacher at the Whittier School, and subsequently at Parkside Elementary School in Camden. Leaving teaching after five years, she took a job in the audit department of the Internal Revenue Service in Philadelphia, working there until retiring in 1988.

Juanita's keen interest in music was fostered by her religious upbringing, and her early exposure to the performance of sacred music in her home and at church. At age eight, her parents, considering it an essential part of her education, provided her with music lessons. Under the tutelage of the distinguished teacher, James Marshall Wheeler, Juanita studied piano and basic music theory. Already singing in the choir, she was asked to play for Chestnut St. UAME's Sunday school at age eleven. The following year, Sue Smith McDonald, a celebrated contralto, teacher, and choral director living in Philadelphia, Pennsylvania, became organist of her church. Following Wheeler's departure for military service, Juanita studied piano and voice with McDonald for five years, at her studio on Ridge Avenue in Philadelphia. In her lessons she played the classics, Methodist hymns, anthems, and spirituals.

During high school and college, Juanita, pursuing her dual interests in piano and voice, performed publicly in a number of venues. Quite proficient as a pianist, she continued to play for her church. Through Sue McDonald's instigation, Juanita sang in the chorus of Philadelphia's Dra Mu Opera Company, the acclaimed black ensemble founded in 1945, for a production of *Carmen*. In addition, McDonald presented her in recitals at several churches in Camden and Philadelphia. When Chris Payne, the organist (and successor of James Marshall

Wheeler) at Camden's Kaighn Avenue Baptist Church, entered military service, Juanita served as his substitute for one year. After graduating from college, she performed in productions of *Cavalleria rusticana* as a member of the McDonald-Wharton Opera Workshop. During her brief marriage in the mid to late 1950's, she was listed in program notices under her combined surname, Fernandez Jones, as when she was accompanist of the Ars Nova Choir of Philadelphia.

In the mid 1960's Juanita joined St. Augustine's Episcopal Church, in Camden. Soon after, she accepted full time, simultaneous appointments, as her church's assistant organist, and as the organist-choir director at Asbury Methodist Church in Pennsauken, playing at 7:30 A.M. and 11:00 A.M., respectively. Sometime later, she took a third position playing at the Mt. Olivet SDA Church in Camden. Juanita, who was hard-working, also held positions at two other southern New Jersey churches: Grace Temple Baptist Church in Lawnside, and New Phillippan's Baptist Church in Camden.

Although principally a church musician in the 1960's, 1970's, and 1980's, Juanita engaged in other musical pursuits. During the 1950's, she had started teaching piano to young children. After becoming a resident of Lawnside, she routinely instructed as many as ten students, presenting them in annual recitals at her church. On occasion, she accompanied vocalists in local concerts. Throughout her career, Juanita maintained a close association with a number of her musical peers, among them Emily Lucken Brown, George Buell, Lois Harris, and Jesse Hamilton, Jr. As a result, she joined the Ecumenical Choir of Camden, New Jersey & Vicinity, an assemblage of the area's leading musicians comprised to honor James Wheeler. On September 10, 1968 in the premier concert, she performed as instrumentalist and chorister. The live recording of the momentous event, produced as an album by Ingram Enterprise, is the only professional documentation of her work.

Gradually losing her sight from the effects of diabetes, Juanita resigned from her positions at Asbury and Mt. Olivet in the mid 1980's, after nearly twenty years of service. However, despite her disability, she continued to play for her own church by memory. In

1993 after suffering a stroke, Juanita retired as organist at St. Augustine's having served for twenty-eight years.

Conspicuous within the ranks of church musicians, Juanita committed herself unselfishly to her calling, even as her health was debilitated in the final years of her career. The source of her life-long dedication was her unceasing love for music. Much respected by all who knew her, she died from the complications of diabetes on November 26, 1995.

FOSTER, ALLEN WILLIAM SR. (b. 1940), pianist, organist, choir director, concert artist, accompanist, composer. The second of three children, Allen was born to Napoleon Nathaniel and Gladys (Allen) Foster in Camden, New Jersey on January 1, 1940. His father, a native of Bellview Florida, was born in 1910. Moving to Camden at the age of nine, he attended public school and graduated from Camden High School in 1927. A talented saxophonist, Allen's father headed a nine piece dance band, Nat and the Bluebirds, that played swing and jazz throughout southern New Jersey. Born in 1917 in Lawnside, New Jersey, Allen's mother was the daughter of a Baptist minister. She was educated in public school, and a 1936 Camden High School graduate. Also a gifted musician, she played piano and oboe. The latter she studied under the tutelage of Dr. J. Maurice Vaughan, a prominent physician who was a charter member and manager of the all-black Hunton Branch Symphony Orchestra, founded in 1921 at the Hunton Branch YMCA in Camden. Allen's brother Nathaniel Thomas, and sister, Ann, also inherited their parents' musical gifts. Tom, who became a prominent attorney, played piano and trumpet. Ann, studied music at Temple University, in Philadelphia, Pennsylvania, then became a dynamic church organist. A very religious family, the Fosters worshipped at Kaighn Avenue Baptist Church, near their home.

Allen received his early education in the Camden public schools. In 1946, after spending one month at the segregated Charles Sumner Public School, he was among the first black children admitted to the H. B. Wilson School. He next attended Cooper B. Hatch Junior High School, and graduated from Camden High School in 1957.

in 1965, earning a bachelor of science degree in business administration. While keeping his post office job, he worked briefly as a substitute teacher in Philadelphia, then took a position as a case worker for the Camden County Welfare Board, in Camden. Following his promotion to a supervisory position, he earned a master of social work degree from Rutgers University, at the New Brunswick campus in northern New Jersey, in 1970. A short time later, he went to work for the School District of Philadelphia, as the supervisor of case work for the Get Set Program, a program for pre-school children.

While still an undergraduate, Allen married Gwendolyn May Winston on June 30, 1963. His wife, notably, became a health educator for the Allegheny Eastern Conference of the SDA Church. Her success as the conference's Director of Health and Temperance led to her conducting a popular radio program and traveling world-wide as a lecturer. Born between 1964 and 1968, their three children were Joya Kim, Allen Jr., and Angela Noell. Upholding the Foster's family tradition, Joya, an excellent pianist and vocalist, earned a degree in music.

Provided with music lessons by his parents, Allen started playing the piano at the age of seven under the tutelage of Catherine Brown, a resident of Bridgeton, New Jersey. Between ages nine and thirteen, he studied with Alice Nix, and Ethel Victoria Howard, both well-known music teachers in Camden. Aided in his development by these capable instructors, Allen quickly demonstrated his great potential as a musician. Since he also loved to sing, within this same period he joined his church's youth choir, directed by Gretchen Branche Waples, a fine coloratura soprano, who worked with her husband, Arthur Waples, in operating a profitable family-owned business as undertakers. (Based in Camden, they served many southern New Jersey communities.)

When Allen was fourteen, he enrolled as a piano student at the Philadelphia Conservatory of Music, at Twentieth and Walnut Streets in the city. Initially placed with Francis Drake, he then came under the tutelage of Jon Carlin, who greatly influenced his playing over a period of three years. As a consequence, his progress was dramatic. Prior to entering the conservatory, Allen had studied organ for two years with Dr. W. Franklin Hoxter, Sr., who was an eminent Philadelphia musician and music teacher. Thereafter, Allen was essentially self-taught. Exposed to a variety of music, he perfected a repertoire comprised of hymns, spirituals, gospel, classics, and jazz.

Obtaining his first position playing for a church at age thirteen, Allen became the pianist of the Pilgrim UAME Church, at Tenth Street and Chelton in Camden. He was paid three dollars a week. In 1955, while performing in a concert as guest accompanist of the Tenth Street Baptist Church's choir, a member of the host church, the Ebenezer Seventh-day Adventist Church of Philadelphia, asked if he would play for its Young Adult Choir. With his parents' permission, Allen accepted the job. Playing there eventually caused him to join the Seventh-day Adventist faith, which he did in 1962.

Because of his increased exposure, Allen received requests to play for other churches. In 1957, he took a second position, as the organist of the Mt. Ephraim Baptist Church, located in the Germantown section of the city. Subsequently, he became the organist-choir director at Pinn Memorial Baptist Church in June of 1960. When Allen came to Pinn Memorial, it had a large music program, with five active choirs. He was responsible for the Sanctuary and Fellowship choirs. The Gospel and Male choruses were directed by Thomasina Johnson James, while the Children's Choir was directed by Nana Dunn. Early in his tenure, Allen broadened the classical repertoire of the Sanctuary Choir, such that they presented Hadyn's *Creation*, Schubert's *Mass in G*, and Stainer's *Cruxifixion*, as well as Handel's *Messiah* and Brahm's *Requiem*. This effort enhanced his success. Later appointed to serve as minister of music, he assumed the added duties of the fiscal management of the music program.

Working closely with musical associates, especially Chris Payne, Jesse I. Hamilton, Jr., and Walter Young, Sr., Allen directed and accompanied joint choirs in the presentation of cantatas and oratorios at several churches in Camden and Woodbury. From the early 1960's, he frequently performed at Mt. Olivet SDA Church in Camden. Four other prominent churches in Camden City hosted these presentations: Kaighn Avenue Baptist, Parkside UM, Tenth Street Baptist, and Wesley AMEZ. Two of the sponsoring parishes were in

73

Woodbury: Bethel AME Church, and Bethlehem Baptist Church. Also a participant in the September 1978 concert of the Ecumenical Choir of Camden, & Vicinity, an association founded in January of that same year to honor fellow musician James Marshall Wheeler, Allen served as one of the instrumentalists.

An accomplished composer and arranger, Allen created his first hymn tune in 1964, entitled *Bradley*. By 1980, he was fully engaged in composing sacred music. Because of this pursuit and his success as a church musician, he was appointed to the SDA Church's nineteen-member Hymnal Committee, the national body that directed the publication of the 1985 edition of the SDA hymnal. Notably, three of Allen's tunes were published in the volume: number 203, *Challenged*; number 298, *Bradley*; number 417, *Finally*. The lyrics set to his music were from established hymns, titled, *This is the Threefold Truth*, *I Lay my Sins on Jesus*, and *O Solemn Thought*, respectively.

Still in his tenure at Pinn Memorial, Allen travels extensively, performing in concert as an organist, and devotes increasing time to composing. A member of the American Guild of Organists, he entered a recent composition in their 1995 hymn competition. Allen is also a member of the W. Russell Johnson Guild, Philadelphia Chapter of NANM, the historic organization founded in Chicago in 1919 by the upper echelon of black musicians, and the Church Musicians Services. The latter, founded by Joyce Drayton Gambrell in Philadelphia, Pennsylvania in the 1980's, is an advocacy group that assists its members with job placements, and seeks higher compensation and better work conditions for musicians. Two other organizations that Allen belongs to are the Alpha Phi Alpha Fraternity and the Academy of Certified Social Workers. Having resumed his study of organ in 1992, he is under the tutelage of Wesley Parrott, of St. Mark's Episcopal Church in Philadelphia.

FRACTION, EDWARD ARTHUR JR. (b. 1939), pianist, organist, choir director, educator, clergyman. Edward Jr., the eldest of four children, was born to Edward and Reba Viola (Paxton) Fraction, Sr. on March 30, 1939. The younger Fraction children were Albert, an equally gifted artist who became a jazz musician, William, and Barbara. From childhood, Edward and his siblings were instilled with a strong work ethic by his parents. During his early childhood, the family, who were deeply religious, attended Ferry Avenue Methodist (later UM) Church in Camden. Although his parents were not musicians, Edward's maternal grandmother, Elsie Paxton, a native of Quantico, Maryland, was a church organist in Glassboro, New Jersey.

By the time he was school age, Edward's musical aptitude was apparent. During first grade at the Charles Sumner Public School in Camden, he started playing the clarinet. Sometime later, after his father bought a piano, Edward taught himself to play it by ear, quickly learning a few songs and hymns. At age ten, he began to play for his church's Sunday school, an opportunity that was crucial in fostering his growth. On one occasion, his embarrassment at not being able to play a particular hymn brought Edward to the attention of Mrs. Fassett, his pastor's wife. Taking an immediate interest in his development, she gave him his first piano lessons, at no charge. After learning to read music under her tutelage, Edward made great progress, a fact that pleased him and his parents.

When he was twelve, Edward's family moved to another neighborhood and left Ferry Avenue Methodist Church. A short time later, he accepted a position, that he kept for two years, as the organist of Mt. Zion ME Church in Woodbury. Because of this additional experience, he was quite proficient by the time he reached his mid-teens.

Inspired by his musical pursuits and, significantly, by his mother, who taught school for thirty-one years, Edward decided to become a music teacher. After graduating from high school in 1957, he enrolled in Glassboro State College (later Rowan College), in Glassboro, New Jersey, majoring in organ and music education. While attending school, he worked in the Camden school district as a substitute teacher. In 1970, immediately after earning his bachelor of arts degree, he entered Trenton State College, in Trenton, to obtain his master's degree. At the same time, he took a full-time teaching position at Camden High School.

Employed for twenty-five years at the school, Edward taught music history, primarily focusing on African American music, and organized the school's first gospel chorus. A stern, but fair disciplinarian, he was respected by his students. Rehearsing during the day and in the evenings, the choir was an amazing success, with 125 members at its peak. Edward, selecting two student assistants, mentored their individual development. Each academic year they presented two concerts. With their reputation spread by word of mouth, Edward and the choir were soon invited to perform throughout New Jersey, and out of state. Maintaining an exciting and hectic schedule of appearances, the gospel chorus performed in other high schools, and various colleges and universities, including Temple University in Philadelphia and the Richard Stockton College of New Jersey, in Pomona. In 1984, after reductions in the school budget, the music program rapidly declined. In 1994, following his two years at Cooper B. Hatch Junior High School, Edward retired from teaching.

From the time he entered Glassboro College, Edward continued his pursuits as a church musician. After joining the Shiloh Apostolic Church in Philadelphia, Pennsylvania in 1957, he served as its organist, intermittently, for many years. In 1962 Edward took a position as the organist-choir director and minister of music of the Second Baptist Church in Atlantic City, New Jersey. Working ten years in this capacity, he played a full-range of music, classical, hymns, Negro spirituals, anthems, and gospel. In addition to serving on Sundays, he and the choir, helping to raise funds for the church, traveled extensively with their pastor. Subsequently, Edward served two Philadelphia churches; he worked three years, from 1972 until 1975, at Nazarene Baptist Church, in the Nicetown section of the city, then accepted a position at the Berean Presbyterian Church, which he held from 1976 until 1992.(An historic black church dedicated November 2, 1884, Berean was founded as the John Gloucester Mission on January 1, 1878 by the Lombard Central Presbyterian Church, likewise an influential African American church.) Highly esteemed for his work with Berean's Chancel Choir and Male Choir, Edward earned a reputation as one of the best organists in the city. Ably assisted by guest artists, such as Robert W. Jones and John Custis, Jr., he successfully presented more rigorous sacred music in concerts, notably Handel's *Messiah*. For his outstanding service and leadership, he was awarded the church's Matthew Anderson Award, named for its first pastor, on October 25, 1987.

Edward, who received his master of arts degree in 1978 from Trenton State College, in Trenton, New Jersey, proceeded to a earn doctorate in sacred music at the Combs College of Music, in Pennsylvania, in 1984. His other musical studies included organ lessons with two eminent musicians, who served two renowned Philadelphia churches. In 1962 he studied with Dr. James E. Hoy, the organist-choir director of Tindley Temple UM Church, formerly the East Calvary ME Church. In 1924, the church was renamed after its celebrated founder-pastor, Reverend Charles Albert Tindley, one of the creators of gospel music. For an additional two years, Edward was under the tutelage of Ronald Cross, the organist-choir director of the First African Baptist Church. (Founded in 1809, its parishioners split into two congregations in 1816. The splinter church's burial ground at Eighth and Vine Streets, and the parent church's burial ground at Tenth and Vine Streets, were the sites of archaeological excavations conducted by John Milner Associates, a Philadelphia architect, archaeology, and planning firm, in 1983–84 and 1990, respectively.)

On rare occasion, Edward performed in individual concerts. Sponsored by his faculty advisor, William Whitehead, he gave his master's recital at the First Presbyterian Church in Bethlehem, Pennsylvania. In Camden, New Jersey, he appeared as the Stevens Street YWCA as the featured guest artist of the *Amateur Hour*, and at Kaighn Avenue Baptist Church.

Edward, because of his association with Dr. Hoy, joined the Philadelphia Association of Organists and Choir Masters, which he described as "Hoy's brainchild." In recognition of his outstanding service as a musician, the Eastern Region of the National Association of Negro Musicians, a division of the prominent organization founded in Chicago, Illinois in 1919, presented him with an award in 1986.

His retirement as the organist-choir director at Berean Presbyterian Church in 1992, prompted in part by the need for back surgery, marked the end of Edward's long career as a church musician. However, he continued teaching music in the Camden School district until June of 1994, when he retired from that career. While satisfied by his work, he expressed great concern about the decline in the study of music in the African American community, "the alarming rate of loss" of church musicians, and in budget reductions in school music programs.

In the fall of 1994, Edward, inspired by his life-long dedication to Christian ministry, enrolled in the Lutheran Theological Seminary of Philadelphia, Pennsylvania. Earning a master of divinity, he graduated May 19, 1996. He now pursues his work in the church as a pastor.

GIVENS, AUDREY CANOIS (b. 1923), pianist, organist, choir director, accompanist, chorister. The seventh of ten children, Audrey was born to George Delano and Amelia B. (Gary) Givens in Camden, New Jersey on April 17, 1923. She and her older sister Thelma, the sixth child, were the only two surviving infancy.

A native of Alabama, Audrey's father was a construction worker and one of the crew that built the Benjamin Franklin Bridge. Spanning the Delaware River and connecting Camden and Philadelphia, Pennsylvania, work started on the structure January 6, 1922 and it opened to traffic July 1, 1926. Also active at church, George served as a deacon and treasurer of their family church, Little Rock Baptist Church in Camden. When Audrey was six years old, he died suddenly, from an illness.

After she was widowed, Audrey's mother, a native of Florida, raised her daughters on her own, supporting them by working as a housekeeper. Musically gifted, Amelia sang on the choir at Little Rock. Every Sunday, because of her mother's deep religious convictions, Audrey and her sister went to Sunday school twice: at their church in the morning; at Wesley AMEZ Church in the afternoon.

Educated in the Camden public schools, Audrey attended the John Greenleaf Whittier School, a segregated grammar school. Completing her secondary education at integrated schools, she was a graduate of Cooper B. Hatch Junior High School and Camden High School, earning her diploma from the latter in 1943.

At the time she started her schooling, Audrey, who was gifted with natural ability, demonstrated a keen interest in music. In the

78

home of Mrs. Queenie Cooper, a neighbor who cared for her and her sister while her mother worked, she started playing the piano by ear, picking out the melodies of favorite hymns and tunes that she sang in church or at school. Heeding the advice of Mrs. Cooper and other friends, her mother gave Audrey piano lessons at age eight. Her first teacher, Charlotte Harvey, was an accomplished member of a distinguished family of Philadelphia and southern New Jersey musicians that included Carl Rossini Diton and J. Harvey Hebron. Audrey studied the fundamentals of music under her tutelage for two years, until Miss Harvey returned to live in Philadelphia. She completed her study of the basics with a Reverend Smith, a local preacher who also taught music.

A creative child, Audrey entertained herself by composing songs and marches. This interest, combined with her mastery of the basics, led her to play marches on the pump organ for the drills of the youth group of the Household of Ruth, affiliates of an Order of Oddfellows in Camden. Singing in the Wesley AMEZ church school choir, directed by Rose Payne Wilson, provided her with an additional rich experience that aided her musical progress.

In 1937, at age fourteen, Audrey began playing for Sunday service at Beulah Baptist Church, a small church on Mt. Vernon Street in Camden. This early opportunity to work as a church musician cultivated her interest in preparing for a professional career. After completing her schooling and securing a job at the Campbell Soup Company, Audrey became a pupil of James Marshall Wheeler, a leading Camden musician, in the mid 1940's. Studying sacred music and secular classics under his tutelage for eighteen years, she developed an expanded repertoire that proved valuable in her later work. Her training included instruction on the organ. In conjunction with her lessons, Wheeler presented Audrey in annual concerts at Kaighn Avenue Baptist Church in Camden, where he served as organist.

By the late 1940's, Audrey, a highly energetic individual, started her active career as a pianist, organist, and choir director. Although she played ten years for the Little Rock Baptist Church's Celestial Choir, she routinely worked in concurrent, short tenure, or part time jobs at small churches in Camden City. By functioning as a substitute organist, Audrey, greatly appreciated for her versatility, provided much needed support to the church community. Following her retirement from the Campbell Soup Company in 1985, she accepted more engagements than in the past, thus maintaining a full work schedule. She has served these churches within Camden: Holy Trinity Baptist Church, Wesley AMEZ, Kaighn Avenue Baptist, Shalom Baptist, Hosanna AME Church, St. Luke's UAME Church, Faith Baptist Church, Chestnut Street UAME Church, Eighth Street UM Church, Mt. Hope UAME Church, and Baptist Temple Church. Occasionally working outside of the city, Audrey has also played for St. Luke's UAME Church in Lawnside, and New Mount Carrie Baptist Church in Philadelphia.

Because her father was a Mason and her mother in the Order of Eastern Star, Audrey, upholding the family tradition, joined the Integrity Chapter, Order of Eastern Star of Camden, where her mother belonged, in 1944. Eventually holding five simultaneous chapter memberships, her singular devotion to the organization was most evident through her prolific work as official pianist for its local, national, and international sessions. Serving in that capacity since the mid 1960's, she provided accompaniment for meetings, special events, such as plays, and conferences. Audrey has served as pianist of the following four southern New Jersey chapters: Integrity Chapter of Camden, House of Jericho; Fiha Court Number Fifteen of Riverside; Primrose Number Nine, Order of the Golden Circle of Camden; Zamora Court, Number One Hundred Thirty Five, Daughter of Isis of Camden. At the national level, she was appointed Assistant Grand Pianist of the Oziel Grand Chapter, Order of Eastern Star of Newark in 1991. Traveling throughout southern and northern New Jersey, Audrey has also played for other branches, by special request. In 1995, another notable achievement was her election as the Royal Commandress of the Madeline Number Four, Royal Court Order of Cyrene chapter in Philadelphia, Pennsylvania.

Early in her career, Audrey instructed a few piano students, that she later referred to James Wheeler. In succeeding years with a constant increase in her playing engagements, she declined to teach music privately. However, as a choir director, she spent a great deal of time training her youth members in basic music theory to improve their performance.

Despite her full schedule, Audrey managed to sing in choirs, a pursuit that she has thoroughly enjoyed. As a member of Kaighn Avenue Baptist Church, she first joined the Chapel Choir in 1949, then the Women's Day Choir in 1976. This facilitated her association with other fine musicians, chiefly Mary Edmonds Burrell and Chris Payne. Likewise, performing in the Ecumenical Choir of Camden, New Jersey & Vicinity, an assemblage of the area's premier musicians formed in 1978 to honor her former teacher, James Marshall Wheeler, was particularly meaningful to Audrey.

Numerous citations from religious, civic, and social organizations highlight Audrey's accomplishments and the high regard of the community for her ongoing dedication. Among the associations that issued her awards are the Order of the Four Chaplains, the Golden Circle Order of Eastern Star, and Kaighn Avenue Baptist Church.

HAMILTON, JESSE IRVIN JR. (b. 1932), pianist, organist, choir director, accompanist, chorister. Third of the four children of Jesse Irvin and Mary (Whittington) Hamilton, Sr., Jesse Jr. was born in Camden on May 7, 1932. His musically gifted family consisted of his father, a prominent organist-choir director and music teacher, his eldest sister Thelma, a vocalist and pianist, and older sister Cornelia and younger brother Paul, both vocalists. Jesse's mother, also exceedingly artistic, was well-known for her recitation of poetry. The Hamilton family, devoutly religious, worshipped at Chestnut Street UAME Church in Camden. Educated in the Camden public schools, Jesse Jr. received his early education in the Octavius V. Catto School, the Charles Sumner Public School, and Cooper B. Hatch Junior High School. Graduating at age seventeen, he completed his secondary education at Camden High School in 1949.

Through his father's influence, Jesse was exposed to a diverse mix of religious and secular music from infancy. At age six, his father started teaching him to play the piano. Under his father's tutelage, his skills progressed sufficiently and he gained a mastery of the fundamentals of music theory. However, when he reached a plateau in his development at the age of twelve, Jesse, through his mother's intervention, stopped playing for more than a year. Two years later, after exhibiting a renewed interest, he started intermediate studies with James M. Wheeler.

In the interim between his lessons with his father and Wheeler, Jesse studied voice with his church's organist-choir director, Sue Smith McDonald, a celebrated contralto, church musician, and among other things, director of the Campbell Soup Male Glee Club. Traveling with his sister Cornelia to her studio in the 2400 block of Ridge Avenue in Philadelphia, he trained with her for a year. Equally important, at McDonald's urging, he and his siblings sang as teenagers in the chorus of the Dra Mu Opera Company of Philadelphia, appearing in *Cavalleria rusticana* and *Carmen*. His lessons, and participation in these renowned professional stage productions fostered Jesse's enduring passion for singing, and his growth as a performer.

While training with Wheeler, who emphasized technical precision and the literal interpretation of music, Jesse received a thorough introduction to the classics. Within a year, he gave his first recital, playing two Beethoven compositions, at the annual meeting of the Philadelphia Music Teachers Association. The event was held at St. Matthew's AME Church (Greater St. Matthew's) in the city. Following his debut, he started performing at community affairs, for teas and funerals. During his second year, Jesse commenced his study of the organ. At this point in his training, he was further influenced by James Allison, a bold and innovative interpreter of music who had succeeded McDonald as organist-choir director at Chestnut Street UAME Church. The contrasting styles of Wheeler, Allison, and his father's were evident in Jesse's unique touch at the keyboard. As he accompanied his mother during her recitations, he was also instilled with an appreciation for the dramatic rendition of lyrics, later manifest in his choral conducting.

Lacking money to pay for college, Jesse enrolled in a printing course at the Camden County Vocational School in 1949. While engaged in his studies, he obtained his first position as an organist, through Wheeler's endorsement, at Zion Baptist Church in Camden. Howard Ways, who directed Zion's choir, appreciably mentored Jesse's maturation as a conductor. By 1951, Jesse became the organist-choir director of Bethlehem Baptist Church in Woodbury. That same year, having completed his course work, he worked briefly for two printing companies.

In 1952, Jesse enlisted in the Air Force and completed his basic training. The next year, he enrolled in technical school at Keesler Air Force Base in Biloxi, Mississippi, and simultaneously, became the organist at one of its four chapels. When stationed in Japan at Misawa Air Force Base in 1953, he initially played as relief to the base organist, and directed the choir. Subsequent to the base organist's return stateside, Jesse was appointed to the position, playing in that capacity for the Presbyterian, Baptist, and Episcopal chapel services, as well as for services at the anti-aircraft batteries. In addition, he became the pianist-director of the Misawa Militaires, an all-male chorus, that performed sacred and secular music on base and in public concerts in various Japanese cities, including Sapporo and on the island of Hokkaido. Joint Easter and Christmas concerts with a Japanese all-female choir were among the Militaires more memorable performances. Upon his return to the United States, Jesse was stationed in Portland, Oregon, where, as base organist, he played for Protestant and Roman Catholic services until his discharge in 1956.

After resuming his printing career, Jesse married Helen Wood of Camden at the Ferry Avenue Methodist (later UM) Church, an historic Camden church, in 1957. Their three children, and especially their daughter, became fine musicians: Vanessa, John, and Jason.

For the next eight years, Jesse declined requests to serve as an organist, feeling somewhat drained from his work in the military. Nevertheless, he engaged in other musical pastimes: singing in his church choir and the Woodbury Choral Society; teaching a few piano students; playing in concert; accompanying vocalists.

In 1965, Jesse accepted a position as the organist at the Parkside Methodist (later UM) Church in Camden. Three years later, he became the organist-choir director, a post that he still holds in the late

1990's. When Jesse started his work, the church had two choirs, the Senior and Junior. Within a short time, he established the Youth Choir, for the teenage vocalists. Eventually, the full complement of choirs grew to six, with the addition of the Male Ensemble, Woodtones Gospel Choir, and Golden Age Choir. Although he initially directed three groups, Jesse concentrated his latter efforts on the Senior Choir, and presenting challenging compositions and arrangements of sacred music. Under his tenure, Wanda Buell, his daughter Vanessa Hamilton, Virginia Bagwell, Sharon Smith, Doris Carpenter, and Isabelle Collins, among others, have assisted him by directing the other choirs. Another unique focus of Jesse's work has been his emphasis on congregational singing, by systematically teaching an unusually large and varied repertoire of hymns to the parishioners. Because of his superb management of the thriving music program, he was awarded the honorary title, minister of music.

Starting in the early 1970's, Jesse collaborated with a number of his peers on elaborate productions of church music in the southern New Jersey community. Featuring a forty-member choir largely comprised of members of Mt. Pisgah AME Church in Lawnside, he and James Allison presented a series of cantatas to packed audiences at Saint Rose of Lima Church in Haddon Heights and the Barrington First Presbyterian Church. Between 1978 and 1981, Jesse played a prominent role as a co-founder and director of the Ecumenical Choir of Camden, New Jersey & Vicinity. The brainchild of Lois Harris, who was minister of music at Wesley AMEZ Church in Camden, the choir was an assemblage of the area's leading musicians in honor of James Marshall Wheeler (1911–1979). Although a huge success, the ensemble disbanded after four years. Thereafter, Jesse worked with Walter Young, Sr., James Allison, and most recently Karen Whitney, in periodical presentation's of Handel's *Messiah*.

In 1970, Jesse left his printing career to work as a salesman for the Black People's Unity Movement (BPUM) Corrugated Box Company. Two years later he enrolled in the Wharton School of the University of Pennsylvania, in Philadelphia, to earn a bachelor's degree in business administration. Taking classes at night, Jesse completed his degree in 1981. After three years at BPUM, he obtained a job at the Johnson and Johnson Company, from which he retired in 1993. Currently a resident of Magnolia, Jesse, who is highly regarded for his accomplishments, maintains his full schedule of musical activities at his church.

HAMILTON, JESSE IRVIN, SR. (1899–1973), pianist, organist, choir director, music teacher, accompanist. The eldest of three children, Jesse was born in Camden, New Jersey, to John Robert and Mary Emma (Still) Hamilton on April 8, 1899. His father was a native of Maryland. His mother, a native of Mount Laurel, New Jersey, belonged to one of the state's famous families; James Still, the Medford doctor, and William Still, author of the *Underground Railroad*, were the most renowned members. Another musical talent, Jesse's sister Corinne became an accomplished vocalist. Their sibling died in childhood. Devoutly religious, the Hamilton family worshipped at Hosanna AME Church in Camden. Receiving his early education in the city, Jesse attended the Octavius V. Catto School, a segregated public grammar school. He completed high school at an esteemed private institution, the New Jersey Manual Training and Industrial School for Colored Youth in Bordentown, New Jersey, known alternately as the Bordentown School.

When he was very young, Jesse's interest in religious music was cultivated by his mother, a church pianist who played for Jacob's Chapel in Mount Laurel, and Hosanna AME Church. After she taught him the basics, he studied piano with three other local music teachers, Bella Morris, Ethel Fox, and Edith Young. At age twelve, he began to play for the Sunday school at his church. Because of his tremendous ability, Jesse was soon assisting the organist. By the time he entered high school, he had secured a position as the organist of Scott's AUMP Church, also in Camden.

During his high school years, Jesse pursued his interest in music, by studying piano, clarinet, and vocal music at the Bordentown school. Through the influence of three of the school's music faculty, he developed an appreciation for a broad range of musical genres. While taking the vocational band instruments course, Jesse came under the tutelage of Eugene Francis Mikell, a distinguished musician, teacher, and composer. Mikell, who was born in South Carolina, commuted to the school by train from his home in New York City. During World War I, he had served as a bandmaster of James Reese Europe's famous World War I 15th Infantry Band of New York. Re-designated the 369th Infantry Band, the unit won numerous accolades in France in 1918. Upon his exposure to band music as popularized by black musicians of the era, Jesse joined a jazz ensemble that played for dances throughout the Bordentown area. Training with two other prominent teachers in the music department also fostered his musical sophistication: Cleota Collins, a native of Chicago and famed vocal concert artist, and Frederick Jerome Work (b. 1877–d. 1942, B. Arts 1903, Fisk University, Nashville, Tennessee, B. Music 1933, Temple University, Philadelphia, Pennsylvania), a noted musician and composer who collaborated with his brother, John Wesley Work II, on the *New Jubilee Songs as Sung by the Fisk Jubilee Singers,* copyright 1901. Their instruction nurtured Jesse's high regard for choral music and opera. Honored by his selection to serve as the chool's student organist at this same time, he performed classical and sacred music in many concerts.

In the early 1920's, after graduating high school, Jesse obtained work at the John Michel's Flour Company. An outgrowth of the Jacob Michel's Sons flour, grain, and seed store, the business was located in the Philadelphia Bourse, a noted commercial center in Philadelphia, Pennsylvania. In a mishap at his job, Jesse severed the ends of his third and fourth fingers on his left hand while operating milling machinery. Despite this lamentable disfigurement, he recovered his dexterity, successfully adapting his fingering technique so that his playing was not affected.

During the late 1920's, Jesse married Mary Whittington, a native of Camden. Their four children, aided by his and his wife's guidance, also became accomplished musicians: Thelma, Cornelia, Jesse Jr., and Paul. Unable to find substantial work with the onset of the Depression, Jesse received government assistance to help support his family until securing a job at the New York Shipyard, in the port of

Playing in the Boys Band of the New Jersey Manual Training and Industrial School for Colored Youth in Bordentown, under the direction of Eugene F. Mikell, fostered the musical growth of Jesse I. Hamilton, Sr., and many other students. This photo shows the 1939 ensemble. New Jersey State Archives, Department of State.

Vocal music was a key part of the Music Department's curriculum at the Bordentown school. The noted musician-composer, Frederick J. Work, who served on the faculty until his death in 1942, organized the Glee Club in February 1920. His successor, Charles Higgins (standing rear center), is pictured with the choral group of 1943. Photo, New Jersey State Archives, Department of State.

Camden, in 1941. Within these same years, he served as the pianist of Asbury ME Church in Pennsauken, New Jersey. At his departure, one of his students, Charles Williams, who belonged to the church, succeeded him.

In 1939, Jesse secured his most prestigious appointment as the pianist-choir director (afterwards organist-choir director) of the Tenth Street Baptist Church in Camden, which he held for thirty-four years until his death. During his tenure, his Senior Choir was among the five largest and most outstanding in the city, a testament to his excellence. Jesse also directed the church's Gospel Choir, and founded and directed the Men's Chorus.

Instructing in excess of two hundred students, Jesse was a highly respected music teacher. His influence was unmistakable on several of his students who later pursued professional careers, among them his own children, and notably, Leon Huff, the co-founder of Philadelphia International Records, in Philadelphia, Pennsylvania. Placing a strong emphasis on theory and finger exercises, he instilled his pupils with the basics, afterwards referring them to other teachers for intermediate and advanced studies. Consistent with his personal preference, Jesse did not present his students in recitals.

Generally appearing in concert only as an accompanist, Jesse was sought after by a number of fine singers and by community organizations. He traveled extensively in New Jersey and Delaware with Katherine Shumake, a noted gospel singer who was the wife of one of the pastors of Little Rock Baptist Church. Holton Hackett, renowned for his work in the Dra Mu Opera Company, was another local singer that Jesse accompanied. Also an early member of the Men's Federation of Camden and Burlington County, Jesse was its official pianist for several years, playing for their large annual events, and monthly breakfasts. In this manner, he gained widespread acclaim as a musician throughout southern New Jersey.

Along with his other pastimes, Jesse was active in a number of fraternal organizations. After joining the Knights of Pythias, Lodge Phoenix Number Five in Bordentown, he held consecutive memberships in the following associations: Pride of Camden Elks Number

Eighty-three; Woodsmen Lodge Camp Number Seven; Hiram Lodge Number Twenty of the FAAY Masons of Camden.

Jesse I. Hamilton, Sr., seated at the keyboard. Photo courtesy of Jesse I. Hamilton, Jr

In 1968, four years after the death of his first wife, Jesse married Mabel C. Darrell, a resident of Plainfield, New Jersey. Fully engaged in his musical pursuits and employed at a local car dealership, he died suddenly in his home in Camden on October 15, 1973. Jesse's funeral at Tenth Street Baptist Church was held October 18, followed by his interment at Sunset Memorial Park in Pennsauken, the next day. At the time of his death, the tributes to his life noted his perpetual joy in playing music and his heartfelt religious devotion.

HARRIS, LOIS CUSTIS (b. 1913), pianist, organist, choir director, accompanist. Lois, one of seven children and eldest of the three who lived past infancy, was born to John and Esther (Ruffin) Custis, Sr. in Norfolk, Virginia in 1913. Both of her surviving siblings, John Jr. and Eunice, also became accomplished musicians.

Lois's parents were natives of Norfolk. Her father, the son of a veteran of the Spanish American War, was awarded a scholarship to attend college. After completing his undergraduate and graduate studies in education and theology at Lincoln University in Oxford, Pennsylvania, he became a Baptist minister and a school principal. To help support himself while in school, he worked as a waiter in Atlantic City, New Jersey, during the summers. Lois's mother, who completed grammar school, high school, and normal school in Norfolk, taught in Virginia's Accomack County. Raised in a very religious family, she attended the Bank Street Baptist Church, in Norfolk, where her father, a trained musician, was the choir director. Also musically endowed, Lois's mother played the piano.

After a ten year courtship, Lois's parents, who met at a Quaker singing-school, were married and settled in Atlantic City. Shortly before her birth, they returned to Norfolk, where her father became the first black principal of the Lott Carey school. By the time Lois was school age, her parents built a house in the town of South Hill, a short distance from Norfolk. After moving there, her father established a Baptist church. Pioneers in modernizing the community, their family was the first to have electricity and a telephone in their home. Her father assisted members of his congregation in doing the same.

As a result of her parents' careers, Lois was educated in segregated schools in Virginia, and in integrated northern schools. At age six, she started grammar school in South Hill, then transferred to her father's school. By the time she graduated from Lott Carey, her father's ill health induced him to resign his position as principal in favor of his Baptist ministry. Within a few months, following his reassignment, her family moved to Portsmouth, New Hampshire. The year was 1924. Lois attended junior high school in Portsmouth, enrolled in classes with white children for the first time. After enduring the cold climate for nearly two years, her parents accepted positions as the headmaster and matron of the Tidewater Institute, a private all-black boarding school established in 1907 in Virginia. However, instead of returning to the South with their mother and father, Lois and her siblings were sent to live with friends in Malden, Massachusetts. When she completed her junior year of high school in Malden, they moved again, to the home of her father's sister, Annie Rabbie, in Philadelphia, Pennsylvania. Finishing her senior year at the Philadelphia High School for Girls, she graduated in 1930. Lois, who found the years of separation from her parents difficult, was happier when living with her aunt and cousins.

In the tradition of her family, Lois's music education began with her exposure to religious music as a small child. Her mother was her first teacher and taught her to play the piano. Endowed with talent, Lois soon began to play hymns at home, often singing with her father as a pastime. Although she developed an interest in jazz as a teenager, her parent's influence was conducive in preserving her devotion to the music of the church.

When she moved to Philadelphia, Lois joined Zion Baptist Church and its seventy-five member Young Peoples' choir. Almost immediately, "Professor" Price, the church's organist-choir director, selected her to serve as accompanist. After his sudden death, Zion Baptist hired Lois as his replacement, paying her a monthly salary of fifteen dollars. Despite her lack of training on the organ, she served dutifully for five years. Within the last two years of her tenure, unexpectedly, the church employed Sue Smith McDonald, a dynamic musician who was a native of Waycross, Georgia, to serve as the choir director. Concerned that her skills were inadequate and had prompted the church to seek another musician, Lois resolved to improve her musical proficiency through advanced study.

In 1936, after her marriage to William Harris, Lois left her position at Zion Baptist Church. Then, pursuing her goal, she studied piano, theory, and harmony under the tutelage of Dr. Borden at the Settlement Music School. Through this association , she secured a part-time position teaching music at St. Simon's Church in the city. At the same time, she founded the Dett Choral Society, an ensemble comprised of thirty young singers and named in honor of the distinguished black composer R. Nathaniel Dett. After months of rehearsals, Lois presented them in concert at the Ethical Society of Philadelphia in 1937. In actuality, since she was pregnant and unable to appear in public, Sue Smith McDonald directed their premiere on her behalf.

Following the birth of her two children, Joan and Edward, Lois pursued a second, more rigorous study of music, by enrolling in the Philadelphia Musical Academy in 1941. During her years there, she took classes in piano, organ, harmony, theory, choral directing, and composition. Her primary instructor was a Dr. Maitland, an excellent teacher who was also a professor at Haverford College. By her own estimation, he profoundly influenced her progress. Attaining a mastery of her craft and armed with a formidable repertoire, ranging from hymns to the classics, Lois was fully gratified by her diligence at the conclusion of her studies.

In 1942, Lois and her family went to live with her parents, who, having retired from the Tidewater Institute, resided at 25th and Diamond Streets in Philadelphia. By then, she had resumed her vocation as a church musician and played for a Baptist church on Norris Street. Subsequent to that position, she served ten years as the organist-choir director of Vine Memorial Baptist Church and two years at Varick Baptist Church. During those years, her work entailed a great deal of travel with her choirs, particularly to revivals, and evening services.

After she and her husband divorced in 1951, Lois also supported her family by working for the federal government. Her first position was at the Veterans Administration, followed by employment at the Navy Depot and the Philadelphia Naval Yard.

Moving to Camden after the death of her parents, Lois became the organist of Wesley AMEZ Church in 1955, as the successor of James M. Wheeler, a revered musician and teacher who resided in the city. At the start of her tenure, the choir was under the very able direction of Rose Payne Wilson, who was also an accomplished contralto. After Wilson's retirement, Lois became the organist-choir director. In her work with the church's four choirs, she often hosted a number of guest ensembles for their ecumenical services. Highly respected and appreciated for her fine artistry, Lois was later honored with the title, minister of music. After giving thirty-eight years of service, she retired in 1993. While working at Wesley, Lois also played for the Mt. Olivet SDA Church in Camden over a twenty-four year period, and substituted at other churches upon request.

The Ecumenical Choir of Camden, New Jersey & Vicinity, a very important assemblage of the area's premier musicians, was the result of Lois's resolve to assist James Marshall Wheeler, after he was stricken with leukemia. Additionally, she desired to promote the performance of complex sacred and classical compositions. Lois's idea was immediately embraced by her peers and she started rehearsing the choir in January of 1978. Among the individuals who had major roles in the organization's evolution were her co-directors, Walter Young, Sr., Jesse I Hamilton, Jr., Mary Morrow, and Vaughn Archie. Representing thirteen churches, the seventy-five voice choir presented its initial concert on September 10, 1978 at Camden High School. The following year, vocalists from forty-one churches participated. In response to Wheeler's wishes, who died November 4, 1979, the choir used its funds to establish the James Marshall Wheeler Scholarship Fund to aid college students majoring in music. After presenting four successful concerts, the organization disbanded in 1982. A live recording of the premier, produced as an album by Ingram Enterprise, is the only professional audio documentation of the ensemble.

Now in her eighties and semi-retired, Lois, who is forthright and quite vigorous, serves the church and the community on a part-time basis. In 1991, she started working at the Christus Lutheran Church in Camden, playing for Sunday services and the vacation bible school. Prior to its closing, she played for its sister parish, the Epiphany Lutheran Church. Lois also substitutes at churches upon request, rehearses the Senior Choir of Kaighn Avenue Baptist Church on the first Saturday of each month, and plays for two funeral homes. A recipient of many citations, she pursues her life-long vocation from her remarkable sense of dedication and great love of music.

HOLMES, ROBERTA JONES (1892–1982), pianist, organist, choir director, music teacher, vocal coach, music retailer. The daughter of

Sallie Jones, Roberta was born at Women's Hospital in Philadelphia, Pennsylvania on June 14, 1892. Within a short time of her birth, her mother moved with her to Newark, New Jersey. While living in Newark, Roberta received her education in the public schools, attending grammar school. When she was sixteen, she and her mother moved to Camden, in southern New Jersey.

Roberta, who was exposed to religious music by her mother, learned to sing hymns and spirituals at an early age. Following her initial informal musical training, she took piano lessons from private teachers, and at the Newark Music School. Through her studies, Roberta learned to play hymns, spirituals, and the classics. Later, she developed an intense passion for gospel music and incorporated it into her repertoire.

A diminutive and high-spirited individual, Roberta began playing for churches, and directing choirs in Newark, in her early teens. After moving to Camden, she became the pianist-choir director of a number of Baptist and Methodist churches in the city. Her most important positions were at Zion Baptist Church, where she and her family were charter members, and Little Rock Baptist Church. During the course of forty-five years, she routinely organized concerts and other programs, to promote the talents of her choirs, students, and all ranks of musicians. One of her greatest contributions was starting the *Back Home Hour* at Zion Baptist Church, the first of its kind in Camden. A weekly songfest and showcase for local talent, it attracted a large audience from many congregations. Because of its popularity, other churches quickly followed suit.

Also within a short time of her arrival in Camden, Roberta married William Cleveland Holmes, a deacon at Baptist Temple Church. They had fifteen children, ten of whom survived past infancy. When her children were very young, Roberta informed them that music was their main interest. She then taught each of them to sing and play the piano. Renowned as choir members at Baptist Temple, Roberta and her offspring performed in concerts, traveling as far south as Wildwood, New Jersey and north to Kingston, New York. By virtue of her training, one son, and three daughters became church musicians: William; Helen; Essie; Mae.

Advertising her services as a music teacher, in the city directory and in black newspapers, such as the *Philadelphia Tribune*, brought Roberta several students from the community. Initially teaching in her home, she eventually conducted her music studios in rented space to accommodate her work. On Saturdays, Roberta gave free classes to neighborhood youths, instructing as many as sixteen students, plus her own children. To encourage her pupils' growth, she presented them in multiple recitals during the year. Among her most talented students was the famed gospel singer Carrie Langford Collier, whom she discovered as a teenager singing in the Camden community.

Simultaneous to teaching, Roberta, who was quite enterprising, operated a highly successful music retail business, called the Universal Music Store. After conducting sheet music sales in her Taylor Street home, she rented a large storefront at 1129 Mt. Ephraim Avenue in Camden and opened a combined retail store and music studio. Able to expand her inventory, she sold pianos as well as gospel sheet music at this location. Roberta's family assisted her in all aspects of the enterprise, including performing selections for customers. Periodically moving, she set up shop at three other sites in Camden: Sixth Street and Kaighn Avenue; in the 700 block of Kaighn Avenue; Seventh and Walnut Streets. Additionally taking her sales operation on the road with the help of her husband, Roberta was a popular vendor at local, regional, and national church meetings and conventions.

In the mid 1950's, Roberta rented an apartment in Newark and opened a music studio, calling it the Universal Music Studio, at Raymond Boulevard and Locke Street. Because she quickly acquired a tremendous number of students, her daughters Essie, Pearl, and Mae helped her to teach. Within that same time, Roberta, who was much sought after as a performer, played at several churches in the city. Commuting to her home in Camden on weekends, she engaged in this venture for four years.

By the 1960's, Roberta stopped playing for churches and focused all of her attention on teaching and performing. Notably, at this time, she entered into a long and rewarding association with Henrietta Fuller Robinson, who was also a dynamic church musician, music teacher, and performer. Upon hearing Henrietta's commercial advertising her musical ventures on WCAM radio, Roberta contacted her and proposed a joint project. As a result, they formed a duo, with Henrietta as vocalist and Roberta as accompanist and dramatic reader. For nearly ten years, they appeared in the city, and in communities such as Atco, Salem, and Mullica Hill. In addition, Roberta and Henrietta recorded a number of popular tunes at a studio on Chestnut Street in Philadelphia, including George Graham's, *I Love Music*, and *Keep Me in the Hollow of your Hand.*

After her eyesight began to fail, Roberta reluctantly retired in her early eighties. Still an active member of the Marian Anderson Music Guild, Camden Chapter of the National Association of Negro Musicians, a chapter of the historic organization founded in Chicago, Illinois in 1919, she was a recipient of its gold plaque award in 1978. Having served her church and community for essentially seventy years with distinction, Roberta died in May 1982.

INGRAM, N. HENRY, SR. (1923–1991), pianist, organist, choir director, accompanist, music teacher, radio broadcast producer and performer, clergyman, politician. The fifth of ten children, Henry, as he preferred to be called, was born to Reverend Joseph Elwood and Laura (Whittington) Ingram, Sr. on Saunders Street in Camden, New Jersey on February 26, 1923. Henry's parents were natives of North Carolina. A Baptist minister, his father pastored two southern New Jersey churches, in Cape May and Keyport. Educated in the Camden public schools, Henry attended grammar school, the Clara S. Burrough Junior High School, and graduated from Camden High School in 1941.

As the son of a minister, Henry was instilled with a love for hymns and spirituals from birth. Musically inclined, both of his parents sang. Henry's older sister Frances, who was a talented pianist, played for their church. Sometime in his early childhood, Henry was taught to play the piano. By the time he was a teenager, he was singing in the choir and playing at Nazarene Baptist Church in Camden. While a student at Camden High School, Henry also sang and played the piano for the school choir.

The same year he finished high school, Henry enlisted in the Navy. A short time later, he married his childhood sweetheart, Vera Henderson, who was the daughter of Reverend and Mrs. Oscar Henderson. After his discharge, Henry and Vera lived in Camden, first briefly with her brother, John Henderson, then in their own home, at 2128 South Seventh Street. The couple had nine children, who developed into exceptional musicians: Frances, Barbara, "Butch" (N. Henry, Jr.), James, William, John, Timothy, Edith, and Virginia. To support his family, Henry worked two jobs, as a special delivery carrier for the U.S. Post Office and as a taxi cab driver.

Proceeding with his musical pursuits, Henry resumed playing for Nazarene Baptist Church. Serving as the organist-choir director for a total of twenty-five years, he conducted three of the church's four choirs, the Senior Choir, Children's Choir, and Male Chorus. In their travels with the pastor, Henry and the members performed throughout New Jersey, in Baltimore, Maryland, and in Washington, D.C. During a short interval in the 1960's, Henry, in addition to his work at Nazarene, played on alternate Sundays for two other congregations in southern New Jersey: Mt. Olive Baptist Church in Magnolia, and Grace Temple Baptist Church in Lawnside.

In the early 1950's, Henry, along with his sister Frances, began singing on the radio program, the *Kershaw Royal Hour,* as a member of the illustrious Kershaw Royal Singers. Founded by Charles V. Kershaw, a resident of Bordentown, New Jersey, the show aired live each Saturday and Sunday morning on station WKDN (later re-named WTMR) in Camden. When Kershaw became seriously ill in the late 1960's, Henry gradually assumed the role of producer-program director. Upon Kershaw's retirement, he took the position fulltime, registering the show with the Federal Communications Commission as *Words and Music.* Under Henry's direction until his death, the program continued to thrive.

Inevitably absorbed in his vocation, Henry joined with his peers in other associations. One very important activity was his membership in the Ecumenical Choir of Camden, New Jersey & Vicinity, an assemblage of the area's leading musicians comprised to honor James Marshall Wheeler, a highly respected Camden musician and teacher. Besides singing in the ensemble, Henry served as its chaplain. When not performing himself, he accompanied vocalists, especially his daughters. Henry also attended the Hampton University Ministers' Conference and Annual Choir Directors and Organists Guild Workshop, a noteworthy inter-denominational body of ministers and church musicians that met jointly at Hampton University, in Virginia, during the month of June. Founded initially as the Ministers' Conference in 1914, the inclusion of musicians started in 1934, with the establishment of the Choir Directors and Organists Guild. From 1973 until 1974, Henry served as president of the latter association.

Sometime in the late 1950's, Henry studied with Napper Henry Hester, III, the eminent organist of Mt. Carmel Baptist Church in Philadelphia, Pennsylvania. While taking his lessons, he arranged with Hester to also teach his children. From the time they were small, Henry, who was their first teacher, insisted that his children learn the fundamentals of music by studying piano, then proceed to playing at least one other instrument. Performing music, at home, in school, and at church, was an integral part of their family life. His efforts led to the creation of a musical dynasty, as each of his children became successful musicians. Henry's daughters attained prominence as soloists and back-up singers for professional acts. His sons achieved national, and international fame as the Ingram Brothers, recording six rhythm and blues albums with a major record label and touring with celebrities, including Patti LaBelle. Entering into music production, they founded Society Hill Records and Ingram Enterprise, recording rhythm and blues and gospel artists. Henry encouraged his sons in their business ventures and provided administrative advice. Significantly, Ingram Enterprise produced the sole concert album, on which he is recorded giving the dedication, of the Ecumenical Choir of Camden, New Jersey & Vicinity.

Late in life, Henry's spirituality led him to fulfill his desire to become a minister. He originally pursued his aspiration in the military, by attending the Southwest Theological Seminary in New Caledonia, in the southwest Pacific. Sometime later, he studied at the Camden Bible Institute. In the mid 1960's, serving as a deacon at Nazarene Baptist Church, where his inspirational speeches earned him the nickname, "Rev", also fostered his interest in the ministry. Resuming his study in the 1970's, Henry enrolled in the Eastern Bible Seminary in Philadelphia. Although very ill at the time, he earned his degree in 1983. He then became pastor of the Bethany Baptist Church in Somerdale, New Jersey, building both a large congregation and a brand new church edifice.

Community service in Camden played a prominent part of Henry's fast-paced life. In the 1970's, he was a member of the Camden Board of Education, the Woodrow Wilson High School Advisory Board, and the A. Phillip Randolph Institute. Holding political office, he was elected to the Camden City Council during the Angelo Errichetti administration.

Highly respected for his achievements and generosity with his time, Henry received numerous awards from local organizations, including more than one commendation as "Man of the Year". His photograph and a very brief biographical sketch of his life was published in Dr. Rebecca Batts Butler's *Portraits of Black Role Models in the History of Southern New Jersey*, Acme Craftsmen Publishers, 1985. A great inspiration to all who knew him, Henry died in Camden on September 12, 1991.

After Henry's death, his eldest son, Butch, became the third producer-program director of *Words and Music.* Because of the show's appeal and large audience, Butch created a televised version based on his father's format, and founded the Words and Music Concert Singers for the project. The television program, also titled *Words and Music,* was broadcast on WGBS Philly 57, a Philadelphia television station, for twenty six weeks in 1992. Although successful in attracting an enthusiastic audience, lack of sponsorship has delayed further production and broadcasts. However, the radio program continues uninterrupted.

JAMES, LOTTIE PRICE (1901–1986), pianist, organist, choir director, music teacher, accompanist. An only child, Lottie was born in

Camden to James H. and Sarah Jane (Trader) Price on December 23, 1901. Three other siblings died in infancy. Her father, who was a native of Parsonsburg, Maryland, worked for the Armstrong Cork Company. A native of Salisbury, Maryland, her mother kept house and earned income by taking in laundry. Several members of Lottie's family were gifted musicians: her father, a trombonist and choir director; her mother, a pianist and music teacher; her maternal grandfather, Solomon Trader, and maternal uncles, George Trader and John Trader, violinists.

Educated in the public schools, Lottie attended the Charles Sumner Public School, the John Greenleaf Whittier School, and the Manual Training and High School (later converted to the Clara S. Burrough Junior High School.) After finishing her secondary education, she entered the Derrick Business School at Fifteenth and Sansom Streets in Philadelphia, Pennsylvania, completing courses in typing and shorthand. Following her training, Lottie worked briefly as a clerk at a real estate business in Philadelphia.

In the early 1920's, Lottie met and married Grover E. James. Of six children born to their union, three survived: Edith, Anna May, Gertrude. After separating from her husband in 1929, Lottie and her daughter's moved to her parents' home. To support her family during the Depression, she obtained work through the Works Progress Administration as a nurse's aide. Thereafter, she earned her livelihood from her musical pursuits.

When she was very young, Lottie's mother started training her to play the piano. After mastering the rudiments, she took lessons from "Madame" Bella Morris, another very exceptional music teacher who served as the organist of Macedonia AME Church in Camden during the first three decades of the 1900's. Provided with an excellent foundation, Lottie learned to play hymns, Negro spiritual, and the classics. Very adept by the age of ten, she played for neighbors weddings and gave her first public recital at her church.

Raised in Ferry Avenue ME Church, founded as Scott's ME Church in 1858, Lottie began to play for its Sunday school at age twelve. During special exercises on Flag Day, May Day, and other patriotic holidays, she often performed military music with the church's eight-member band, among who were Albert Sprittles, the founder-director, her father on trombone, William Gunby on cornet, and Miss McPherson Jones (later Cooper) on violin. A year or two later, becoming the pianist of her church additionally nurtured her musical progression. After the church installed a pipe organ, Lottie, in order to master the instrument, studied with Amelia Hawks Thorne, at the Theodore Presser School of Music in Philadelphia.

By the early 1920's, Lottie started teaching piano and voice in her home. As more churches purchased organs, she was also engaged to train their pianists, and to perform at the formal installation of the instrument. Lottie's increased public exposure enhanced her reputation, and rapidly afforded her more work. Several of Camden's leading church musicians came under her tutelage at an early age; among this group were Elmira Howard Davis, her successor at Ferry Avenue Church, James Marshall Wheeler, Theodore H. Brooks, and James R. Allison.

From the mid 1930's until the mid 1970's, Lottie, served as the organist of St. Bartholomew's Roman Catholic Church in Camden. Eventually converting to Catholicism, she was confirmed as a member of the church in 1952. At the same time she played for the parish of St. Bartholomew's, she held secondary appointments at a succession of four Camden churches: Bethel AME Church, Union AME Church (UAME denomination), Pilgrim UAME Church, and Tenth Street Baptist Church. She also served St. Matthew's Union Church in Merchantville, and Ezion Church in Wilmington, Delaware. Simultaneous to her church work, Lottie played for the Walker Funeral Home in Camden, continued to teach, and accompanied several singers in concert.

After forty years of intense activity, Lottie retired from virtually all of her rewarding pursuits. Then, during the last ten years of her life, she devoted herself to the Marian Anderson Music Guild, Camden Chapter of the National Association of Negro Musicians. This chapter was an affiliate of the historic national organization in Chicago, Illinois, founded by the upper echelon of black musicians in 1919. She performed regularly in NANM concerts, and served in elected office: corresponding secretary from 1980 to 1982; second vice-president from 1983 to 1986. Because of her outstanding career, Lottie received the chapter's 1982 gold plaque award.

Living with her daughter Edith, Lottie's last residence was at Northgate Towers in Camden, New Jersey. She died on May 12, 1986.

KING, BETTY JACKSON (1928–1994), pianist, organist, choir director, music teacher, composer, educator. The daughter of the Reverend Frederick Douglas and Gertrude (née ?) Jackson, Betty was born in Chicago, Illinois in 1928. Her father was the founder and pastor of the People's Community Church and Center of Woodlawn. A highly talented musician, Betty's mother was the founder-director of the Imperial Opera Company and the Jacksonian Institute.

Under the tutelage of her mother, Betty's musical education started when she was very young. Exceedingly precocious, she began to accompany her mother's choirs and compose arrangements of Negro spirituals, at ages nine and eleven, respectively. By the time Betty was a teenager, her mother, her sister Catherine, who became a prominent soloist and choir director, and she were performing as the Jacksonian Trio, in concerts at churches and educational institutions throughout the midwest and southern regions of the country. In later years, the effects of her religious upbringing and love for sacred music was quite evident, as the majority of her arrangements and compositions featured Negro spirituals and biblical themes.

Educated in the public schools of Chicago, Betty graduated from high school in 1946. In pursuit of her post-secondary studies, she enrolled in the Chicago Musical College of Roosevelt University, majoring in piano and minored in organ. Upon receipt of her bachelor of arts degree in 1950, she entered the college's graduate program. In 1952, she earned her master of music in composition, with a minor in voice. During these years, Betty was influenced by her expert instructors, most significantly, Joseph H. Lockett, Thelma Waide Brown, Esther Goetz Gilliland, and Dr. Hans Tischler. Lockett, of particular interest, was a native of Philadelphia, Pennsylvania, receiving his training and establishing his career as a church musician, concert artist, and music teacher in the city before relocating to the Midwest in the 1940's. Over a period of several years, Betty pursued

103

post-graduate studies at several institutions: Oakland University, Oakland, California; the Peabody Institute, Baltimore, Maryland; Bank Street College, New York City, New York; New York University; Edwards College, Mississippi; Glassboro State College, Glassboro, New Jersey; Westminster Choir College of Princeton University, Princeton, New Jersey. Her extensive academic preparation, in fact, was a key determinant of her exceptional career success.

From the mid 1950's until he early 1990's, Betty, who was widely respected for her genius and professionalism, engaged in a full complement of noteworthy activities as a teacher, conductor, concert artist, accompanist, lecturer, and composer. Because of her expertise, she worked simultaneously in local and national spheres. Devoting more than thirty years to teaching, Betty's initial faculty appointments were in Chicago at Roosevelt University and Dillard University. She also taught at the University of Chicago Laboratory School and the Jacksonian Institute. During the early years of her career, she served as the accompanist for the Northwestern University Theater, the Merchandise Mart Chorus, and the Chicago Umbrian Glee Club. She directed the Pre-Professional Choral Ensemble, and the Congregational Church of Park Manor Choir.

After becoming a resident of Wildwood, New Jersey, Betty spent a total of eighteen years in secondary education at the Wildwood Junior and Senior High Schools, from 1976 through 1974 and 1976 through 1989. By teaching and directing music classes, vocal and instrumental ensembles, and stage productions, she educated nearly 4000 students. Cited for excellence upon her retirement, she was the recipient of the Governor's Teachers Recognition Award for the State of New Jersey.

Betty, with an extremely demanding schedule, additionally was the choir director of St. James AME Church in Atlantic City, and the King Singers, a group she founded in Wildwood. Besides working as a director, she served as the accompanist of the Grace Notes Choral Ensemble of the Riverside Church in New York City.

In promoting the work of African-American music and musicians, particularly in the genres of classical and sacred music, Betty traveled extensively, lecturing and conducting music festivals at several institutions. Her most significant programs were at the following places: University of Ohio; the University of Minnesota; the Alabama Center for Higher Education; Jackson State University; University of California (San Diego); Delaware State University; Allen AME University; South Carolina State College. As a result of her overwhelming commitment, she was enlisted as an adjudicator, conductor, concert artist, and clinician in programs given by other sponsoring organizations. This interest also led Betty to become a lifetime member of the National Association of Negro Musicians, the organization founded in Chicago in 1919 by musicians of her caliber. More important, she served as the organization's national president from 1979 until 1984. During those years, she maintained close ties to the members of its southern New Jersey affiliate, the Marian Anderson Music Guild, Camden Chapter of NANM, in Camden, New Jersey.

A prolific composer and arranger, Betty created in excess of 100 keyboard, vocal, and instrumental works. Several she published through Hope Publishers, Somerset Press, and Belwin Mills, established publishing houses. Later, she published and marketed her compositions through her own business venture, the Jacksonian Press. Her compositions were quite varied genres: two biblical operas, *Saul of Tarsus* and *My Servant Job*, an Easter cantata, *Simon of Cyrene,* a requiem for full chorus and soloists, a ballet, *The Kids in School and Me, Nuptial Suite, Four Seasonal Sketches, Aftermath, Dawn of Compensation, Life Cycle for Soprano, Cello, and Piano, Berceuse for Violin and Piano, Vocalise, A Lullaby for You, Calvary,* and several solo and choral arrangements of Negro spirituals. Besides Betty's inclusion of her compositions in concert programs, a number of her peers performed her works. One such occasion was Mary Winston-Smith's performance of *Calvary,* at Zion Baptist Church in Philadelphia, Pennsylvania for the June 1987 Gala Memorial Concert of Opera Ebony, a prestigious black vocal ensemble. Betty's 1990 arrangement of *Go Tell It On The Mountain* was dedicated to and performed by LaNetta Desrosiers and the First Methodist Church Choir of Cape May Court House, New Jersey. A recent commercial use of her compositions was in a 1994 recording on compact disk by the vocal quartet, Videmus; produced by Koch International Classics, the collection, entitled, *Watch and Pray: Spirituals and Art Songs by African-American Women Composers* includes Betty's *Springtime*, and her arrangements of two spirituals, *Calvary* and *It's me, O Lord*. The recording featured several works of four other composers: Julia Perry, Undine S. Moore, Margaret Bonds, and Florence Price.

Betty belonged to the American Women Composers, the American Choral Directors Association, the Music Educators National Conference, and the New Jersey Music Educators Association. She received key awards for her regional contributions: the "Contemporary Woman" award of station WYVR in Pomona, New Jersey; the NAACP Cape May County Award; citations from the Wildwood Board of Education. Brief biographic entries are listed in: *American Black Women in the Arts and Social Sciences; International Who's Who in Music; Black American Music; Choral Music by African-Americans; the Biographical-Dictionary of Afro-American Musicians; New Jersey Educators Association Professional Development Institute*. Specific edition dates of these volumes are unknown.

After a serious illness, Betty died in New Jersey in June of 1994. Surviving relatives included her ninety-one year old mother, Gertude Jackson Taylor (re-married after first husband's death). Funeral services were held in Chicago, at the Metropolitan Community Church. A memorial service was also held by her daughter, Rochelle Johnson, at the Christ Gospel Church in Middle Township, New Jersey.

LITTLE, J[ESSE] FERMAN (b. 1920), pianist, organist, choir director, accompanist, composer, clergyman. The only child of Anthony and Katie (Robinson) Little, Ferman was born in Greenville, South Carolina on March 22, 1920. His father, a World War I veteran, died when he was an infant. A native of Newberry, South Carolina, Ferman's mother was an accomplished church musician, playing both the piano and pump organ.

When he was four years old, Ferman and his mother moved to the Northern Liberties section of Philadelphia, Pennsylvania. Educated in the public schools, he entered the Paxon and James Madison Elementary School. After his mother married William Henry Washington, Ferman moved to Newport News, Virginia, where he attended the John Marshall Elementary School from 1931 until 1933. Later that same year upon the death of his step-father, he and his mother returned to Philadelphia. Subsequently re-enrolling in the public schools, he graduated from Phillip Kearney Junior High School, and attended the Central High School for Boys, at that time located at Broad and Green Streets. Being very religious, his mother and he attended several small churches, oftentimes where she served as a musician.

As a result of his mother's influence, Ferman was enthralled with music from the time he was very small. At first, his attention was focused exclusively on singing. However by the age of nine, Ferman became fascinated with his mother's playing, and asked her to teach him. Pleased with his great interest, she immediately started instructing him on the pump organ. His lessons, combined with performances in school and at church, soon revealed his considerable musical and dramatic talents.

When Ferman was thirteen and once again living in Philadelphia, he took piano lessons under the tutelage of a Professor Ross, who lived in the 1800 block of North Van Pelt Street. The fifty cents that he earned working weekends on the delivery trucks of the Nu Process Laundry, where his mother was employed, paid for his lessons. Mrs. Zetta Gordon, a teacher at a local church center who took a special interest in him, also helped nurture his growth by giving him a bible and his first piano. In the midst of his studies, Ferman, who was very astute, started teaching the rudiments of piano to neighborhood teenagers. Before long, he obtained a position playing for the Calvary Baptist Church. Meanwhile engaged in his vocal pursuits at Central High School, Ferman received noteworthy praise for his baritone rendition of *Water Boy*, the composition made famous by Paul Robeson. Likewise, a successful vocal audition led to his appearance on the Major Bowes radio program, at a local station.

By the time he was sixteen, Ferman's pursuance of his musical and religious interests effected his interaction with the local Radio Church of God and Bible School, a branch of the national broadcast church founded and directed by the famous radio preacher, Elder Lightfoot Solomon Michaux. Quickly engrossed attending services

107

each night, he stopped studying, dropping in rank from the top four in his class to failing. Consequently, he was expelled in the middle of his junior year.

Ferman's expulsion effected a momentous change in his life. At the age of seventeen, after writing and receiving an invitation, he moved to Washington, D.C. to work directly with Michaux. Shortly after his arrival, Ferman, noticeably refined and dignified in his manner and speech, became the official bible reader during the Pastor's radio broadcasts and local evangelistic sermons. Besides performing this function, he served as the director of the church's renowned 156 voice Cross Choir. In their extensive travels over a period of nine years, he was also featured as a baritone soloist. Well-versed in music, he performed a great stock of hymns, spirituals, gospel, and sacred classics. Receiving national acclaim, the Cross Choir attracted the attention of several celebrities, such that, at one of the choir's memorable performances in Town Hall in Philadelphia, Gene Autry was present. Through more than ten years with Elder Michaux, Ferman met many other personages, most notably Eleanor Roosevelt and Mary McLeod Bethune. Within that period, while fulfilling his musical duties for the Radio Church of God, he periodically studied for the ministry.

In March of 1941, Ferman married Mary E. Ruffin, who was a member of the Cross Choir and a dramatic reader. A native of Wilson, North Carolina, she was raised in Washington, D.C. In the ensuing years, Ferman routinely accompanied his wife in her vocal and monologue presentations. Their joint performances were well-received and they appeared for many years at churches in locales along the coast of the eastern United States, including southern New Jersey.

While serving four years in civilian public service during World War II, Ferman, with hopes of pursuing a vocal career, studied voice with Alice Harrell of Newark, New Jersey. However, subsequent, unsuccessful auditions for professional jobs in New York City halted his aspiration. Instead, through an association with highly skilled musicians in that same period, Ferman turned his attention to composing hymns. In 1948, he published *Let the Drop From Heaven Fall On Me*, in collaboration with his wife, who wrote the lyric, and Mary E. Lacy Moore, who harmonized and arranged the work.

After leaving the District of Columbia and returning to Philadelphia in 1949, Ferman secured positions playing for the Church of God at Fifty-first Street and Haverford Avenue, and the York Street Church of God. Then, following years of study, he was ordained a minister in the First Church of God Reformation in 1956.

Subsequently moving to Camden, Ferman founded the First Church of God, at 735 Chestnut Street, in 1956. Since his small congregation was at most forty-five families, they could not afford a full time musician. As a result, he played for services and directed the choir for more than thirty years, until his retirement in 1986.

Due to his desire to promote the performance of religious and classical music, Ferman co-founded the Camden Chapter, later renamed the Marian Anderson Music Guild, of the National Association of Negro Musicians. The parent organization was founded in Chicago, Illinois in 1919, by the foremost black musicians in the concert world. At the suggestion of his associate, Reverend Calvin N. Delph, who was a Church of God minister and NANM member, he established the branch in 1971, with Isabelle M. Collins. A great lyric soprano who resided in Camden, she was one of the organization's chapter establishment representatives. Serving as the first president, then as vice-president, Ferman hosted the NANM meetings, concerts, and anniversary programs at his church from 1971 until 1982. He additionally performed in several of their programs. Another factor very important to him, this undertaking allowed him to encourage the talents of several young musicians in southern New Jersey.

While employed by the Department of the Navy, Ferman earned his General Equivalency Diploma, thirty years after leaving high school. He completed his undergraduate education at Rutgers University, in Camden, graduating with a bachelor of arts degree in psychology in 1981. Ferman then earned a master of arts in pastoral counseling from LaSalle University in Philadelphia, Pennsylvania, in 1987. After working six years as a substance abuse counselor in Mount Holly, New Jersey, he retired.

Ferman and his wife are the parents of six adopted children. Actively composing sacred music, he performs and records his works on a KORG electronic digital keyboard.

MCDONALD [WIMBISH], "SUE" [SUSIE SENORA] SMITH (1901–1997), vocalist, concert artist, pianist, organist, choir director, music teacher, accompanist, musical director. Born July 1, 1901 in Waycross, Georgia, Sue was the daughter of John and Maggie (Smith) Hogan. When still very young, at the inducement of her grandmother and namesake, Susie Smith (a.k.a. "Aunt Sue"), she was adopted by her mother's sister and brother-in-law, Mary (Smith) and Jenkins McDonald. Receiving her early education in the public schools, Sue graduated from Waycross High School in 1915. The following year she received a general elementary teacher's certificate and started teaching in the school district. Sometime in the 1920's, Sue married Hugh Wimbish, a dentist. Tragically, both he and their son, who was an only child, died a short time later.

From early childhood, music was an integral part of Sue's life. While growing up, she was fundamentally influenced by her grandmother, whose charismatic singing kindled the religious fervor of the congregation of the St. Peter's Baptist Church in Waycross. By the time Sue was a teenager, she was herself a dynamic vocalist and pianist. From her own desire to pursue music as a career and her grandmother's encouragement, she entered Clark University in Atlanta as a music major, where she received a diploma in 1920, and a bachelor of arts in 1923. Subsequently, she studied piano and voice at the Chicago Conservatory of Music, in Chicago, Illinois, earning her master of arts.

Upon the receipt of her credentials, Sue taught at two southern colleges, affiliates of the Methodist Church, between the mid 1920's until 1930. She spent two years at Walden College, in Nashville, Tennessee, and four years teaching voice in the music department of Claflin College, in Orangeburg, South Carolina. The latter, founded in 1869 by the Freedmen's Society of the Methodist Episcopal Church, consisted of a liberal arts college, a normal school, and secondary (college preparatory and domestic arts) and elementary divisions. During her tenure at Claflin, her artistic direction of the Claflin Col-

110

lege Quartette brought her wide-spread recognition in collegiate circles throughout the region. At the same time as her teaching, Sue, who was a fine contralto, worked as a church musician and appeared in concert in several venues.

After moving to Boston, Massachusetts in 1930, Sue, with hopes of embarking on a successful career as a concert artist, entered the Boston Conservatory of Music, studying voice under the tutelage of Jessie Fleming Vose. While engaged in her studies, she directed the Mansfield Singers, a local choral group. After sometime, she attracted the attention of individuals in the elite of the music world. Significantly, Sue was befriended by Mrs. Roland Hayes, who then introduced her to Roland Hayes. Her fine training and her prestigious Boston affiliations were considerable assets in her later professional pursuits.

When Sue moved to Philadelphia, Pennsylvania in 1932, she opened her own music studio to give private instruction in piano and voice. Although she intended to stay only a brief time, her gratifying work, especially with children, persuaded her to make the city her permanent home. Through her dynamism, Sue attracted a large number of students from Philadelphia and New Jersey. Publishing these words of advice for her pupils on a promotional leaflet, she wrote:

> "As one who has served and counselled some of you, wept, worked and quarreled with you, let me again remind you as of old, 'There are no short cuts.' 'If you must listen to applause, keep your heads lifted, your eyes forward. Applause can become loud and mocking if one permits the head to turn.'…'May you prove worthy of your gift, remembering that a setting of humility and sincerity enhances the brilliance of Your Jewel."

Sue gave her student's many opportunities to perform, in recitals and as part of her own ensembles, such as the McDonald Singers, the Haven Vested Four (later five), and the Wharton-McDonald Choral Ensemble. When Raymond Lowden Smith founded the Dra Mu Opera Company of Philadelphia in the mid 1940's, she joined the board of directors for a brief period and sent her most talented pupils to perform in productions as members of the chorus. For more than forty years, Sue conducted her studio at four North Philadelphia locations: 2527 West Oxford Street; 2400 West Columbia Avenue; 2444 Ridge Avenue; 1821 West Tioga Street.

While teaching was the inception of her professional career in Philadelphia, Sue quickly became prominent through a prolific assortment of activities. Still engaged as a concert artist, she continued her personal training with Louis Shenk, who was a respected vocal coach. Later, under the tutelage of Tilly Barmach, Felice d'Antbourg Wolmut, and Hans Wolmut, she extended her vocal range from contralto to mezzo-soprano and dramatic soprano. From 1933 through the mid 1950's, Sue was presented in numerous concerts at the Ethical Society of Philadelphia and at various churches. In 1936, she was the featured soloist for the annual concert of the E. Gilbert Anderson Memorial Symphony Orchestra, the distinguished all-black orchestra under the direction of Raymond Lowden Smith. In the 1940's and 1950's, Sue was a soloist at Gimbel's Department Store, performed regularly in New York City, and conducted tours of the southern colleges. Notably, while performing in summer stock, Sue met Ethel Waters, who became her student and very good friend. As a result of this association, she traveled to Hollywood to serve as the musical director for a show that starred Waters, who called her "Susie Q" and introduced her as "my educated friend." Sue met other prominent African American artists, including Hall Johnson, the violinist, violist, choir director, and composer, who performed with his choruses in a number of Broadway and Hollywood musicals.

After arriving in Philadelphia, Sue served as the choir director or organist-choir director of several of the city's churches: Mt. Olivet Tabernacle Baptist Church, Zion Baptist Church, Salem Methodist Church, Haven Methodist Church, and Tioga Methodist Church. She also played in Ardmore, Pennsylvania, for Zion Baptist Church. Sue's other important work was at the Wharton Settlement House, located at 1706–1708 North Twenty-second Street. Employed there for more than twenty years, she conducted the adult and children's piano department and directed four ensembles: the Whartonettes, the Marian Anderson Glee Club, and the Wharton Singers. The latter was comprised of two groups, the Male and Mixed Choruses, one performing in concert, the other on radio broadcasts.

By the mid to late 1930's, Sue had expanded her work into southern New Jersey. She accepted positions in Camden at the Chestnut Street UAME Church, Nazarene Baptist Church, and the Union AME Church (UAME denomination) and performed in church-sponsored

Sue Smith McDonald, in 1950's photo,
by David King. Courtesy of Eva P. Jester.

concerts. Operating in this sphere brought her an exceptional opportunity. Because of her expertise, Hyland Frisby, who was a Campbell Soup Company employee, recruited her to direct a newly formed ensemble that he managed and the company sponsored.

Dedicated to performing for the benefit of World War II military personnel and veterans, Sue and the Campbell Soup Male

● STEADY, IT'S A TAKE! And the recording begins. The Campbell Male Chorus, one of the best groups in this area, record "The Red Cross Song" and "The Lord's Prayer." Mrs. Sue McDonald directs. Front row, left to right: Leon Jenkins, Third Floor retorts; Clifton Brown, Fifth Floor raw chicken; Thomas Freeman, No. 2 Plant retorts; Munnger Hyland Frisby, Control Laboratory; Alexander Barber, Fifth Floor raw chicken; Lloyd Mitchell, Fifth Floor Digesters; John Byrd, formerly of Fourth Floor raw chicken; Raymond Cox, Seventh Floor Cafeteria Steward.

Back row, left to right: James Hinton, Second Floor Labeling; Robert Schaeffer, No. 2 Plant retorts; John Jackson, Control Lab; James Ingram, Fourth Floor celery operation; Elwood Stafford, Third Floor Research Lab; John Moody, Second Floor Labeling; Lewis Stokes, No. 2 Plant filling; John Brown, Elevators.

How to Make a Record . . .

Glee Club met for their first rehearsal on November 17, 1942. Thereafter, they practiced twice weekly, at the plant and in her Ridge Avenue studio, except during tomato season, the peak summer work period. With a complement of twenty-eight singers, Sue and the members gave their first concert on January 5, 1943 at the Campbell Soup Company's Foreman's Club. In their inaugural year, the ensemble performed throughout the city: Campbell Employees Federal Credit Union; Union AME Church; a Baptist church at 9th and Van Hook; Bethel AME Church; St. John's Baptist Church; Bethel Methodist Church; Tenth Street Baptist Church. Their concert schedule also included performances at Bethel AME Church in Moorestown, Macedonia Baptist Church in Delaware Township (Cherry Hill), Victoria Methodist Church in Westville, Asbury Methodist Church in Pennsauken, and at four Philadelphia churches.

These photos of the Campbell Soup Male Glee Club, printed in the in-house publications of the Campbell Soup Company, in Camden, New Jersey, are two in a large series documenting their twenty year career.

Top left: Onstage, during an American Red Cross sponsored show at the Valley Forge General Hospital, Valley Forge, Pennsylvania, October 16, 1945. (The Wharton-McDonald Chorus (female) also performed that day.) The November 1945 'Soup Tureen' photocaption listed the members' names, but did not identify their positions in the picture. Those present were John Byrd, Clifton Brown, Raymond Cox, J. B. Coney, Hyland Frisby, John E. Gray, Roland Hall, John Jackson, Leon Jenkins, John Moody, Robert Stafford, Elijah Williams, Alexander Barber, Charles Campbell, Edward Jenkins, George Riley, James Hinton, and Samuel Benson. Three names were omitted. Photo, by Leon Drost, courtesy of Eva P. Jester.

Bottom, left: Sue Smith McDonald conducting the chorus in their April 1953 recording session at WIP Radio Station in Philadelphia. Published May 1953 in 'Campbell People.' Reprint from the Campbell Soup Company Archives, Camden, New Jersey.

For twenty years, Sue and the Campbell Soup Glee Club, later known as the Campbell Soup Male Chorus, continued a full schedule of fifteen to twenty annual appearances. During that time, the American Red Cross and the USO (Uniformed Services Organization) hosted many of the ensemble's memorable concerts at Fort Dix, in Wrightstown, New Jersey, and the Valley Forge General Hospital, in Valley Forge, Pennsylvania. Performing on radio in Department of Defense's programs at Philadelphia stations WCAU, WPEN, WIP brought them national acclaim. In 1953, they achieved greater prominence after recording the national theme song for the American Red Cross, written by Maryann Monahann, who was the sister of a Campbell Soup employee. Engineered by Robinson Recording Laboratories at WIP's studio, the record consisted of Sue's arrangement of Monahann's tune, and the choirs rendition of the Lord's Prayer on the reverse. After dwindling to twelve members, the Campbell Soup Male Chorus disbanded in the early 1960's.

In the early 1950's, Sue recruited a majority of the Campbell Soup Male Chorus to perform in opera productions with her Wharton-McDonald Choral Ensemble. Later changing the name to Wharton-McDonald Opera Workshop, she listed the male chorus under separate billing. In 1953, after receiving permission from Gian-Carlo Menotti, the renowned composer, Sue staged the first production by a local black company of his famous opera, *Amahl and the Night Visitor.* The Wharton-McDonald Opera Workshop presented its repertoire of popular works, including *Cavalleria rusticana,* in Philadelphia, New Jersey, Delaware, and Maryland. One of their southern New Jersey performances of *Cavalleria* was sponsored by the St. James AME Church in Atlantic City, and held at the New Jersey Avenue School on May 5, 1960. A second noteworthy performance was sponsored by the Macedonia Baptist Church of Cape May, for the 32nd Annual Hotel and Guest Program on August 24, 1961 at Convention Hall in Cape May. Among the group's primary soloists were Eva P. Jester, Susan Foster Smith, Helen Rose Stewart, Carrie Eldridge, Mary A. Dancy, William E. Smith, Hyland Frisby, Elwood Stafford, Jimmy Brice, Jr., Jesse Scott, Jr., Anderson B. Bryant, Richard Stafford, and James R. Moore. When serving as the organist-choir director of

116

Tioga Methodist Church in the mid 1960's, Sue also presented *Pagliacci* with its choir. Under her direction, the Wharton-McDonald Opera Workshop remained active into the early 1970's.

Renowned for her life-time achievements, Sue's greatest accolades were given her at two special occasions. The first, the silver anniversary celebration of the Sue Smith McDonald Music Studio, was sponsored by the Bright Stars of Haven Methodist Church, at Twenty-third and Oxford Streets in Philadelphia. Her second grand tribute, from the Pro Arts Society of Philadelphia, was held at the city's Bellevue Stratford Hotel on February 25, 1973. On that occasion, she and W. Russell Johnson, an equally accomplished musician, were feted by their peers and students. Gradually reducing her activities, Sue retired in the early 1980's.

In the late 1980's, Sue moved to Simpson House, a Philadelphia retirement community and affiliate of the Eastern Pennsylvania Conference of the UM Church. Playing in the center's programs well into her nineties, she amazed all with her joyous performances. Eva P. Jester and Elfreda Fassett, former students who managed her business and legal affairs, visited faithfully. Sue died on January 26, 1997.

OUTLAW, LAURA BEEKS (1921–1994) pianist, organist, choir director, accompanist. One of two children, Laura was born in Philadelphia on March 10, 1921 to John Westley and Mary (née ?) Beeks. Musically gifted, her mother was a pianist, choir director, and a vocalist. When she was very young, Laura's family moved to Berlin, New Jersey. She attended the segregated East Berlin Community Grammar School, and graduated from the Haddonfield Memorial High School. In the mid 1940's, Laura moved to New York City became a clerical worker. After completing a course of study at the Washington Business Institute, she eventually secured a position in the Mayor's Office of the Borough of Manhattan, from which she retired after working twenty-two years.

Laura's innate love of music derived from her mother's influence. Under her mother's tutelage, she learned to sing and play the piano at an early age. Because of her aptitude, Laura's mother sent her for more advanced studies with Edna Reybold, a resident of Clementon, an adjacent town, and later, Louis Parson, who resided in Berlin. In her early teens, at the recommendation of Parson and with her mother's encouragement, Laura became organist of her church, the Greengrove Baptist Church, founded in 1925. After Reverend Hurst, the pastor of White Oak Baptist Church in Lindenwold requested her services, she played for both on alternate Sundays.

During her years in New York City, Laura continued her musical pursuits, while simultaneously engaging in new artistic endeavors. In appearances at several churches, she performed as a concert pianist and as a member of choirs. Motivated by her interest in acting, Laura completed studies in drama and modeling at the New York Academy of Fine Arts. Later, her theatrical talent won her a role in an off Broadway production of *Little Women.*

Sometime between the late 1960's and early 1970's, Laura returned to Berlin and commuted to her job in New York. Not long after her arrival, she began to perform at area churches and in other settings. After renewing her membership in Greengrove Baptist Church, she played there occasionally. Once she retired, Laura especially devoted many years to providing musical entertainment for senior citizens. As a member of the Keenagers Senior Citizen Group at the Open Bible Baptist Church in Williamstown, Laura played for their monthly Community Service Talent Show. While serving as an RSVP volunteer at the Archway Medical Daycare Center for Adults in Atco, she delighted the residents with her piano renditions of familiar music. In the early 1980's, Laura joined the Marian Anderson Music Guild, Camden Chapter of the National Association of Negro Musicians. A very dedicated member, she served as its treasurer from 1983 until her death. A participant in chapter sponsored concerts, she performed at the Walt Whitman Center for the Arts in Camden and at Grace Temple Baptist Church in Lawnside. Maintaining a full agenda of musical activities, Laura additionally accompanied a youth choir that performed in the Berlin area.

Quite energetic, Laura lent her considerable talents to other noteworthy activities. Politically active, she served in three Democratic organizations on Staten Island: North Shore Democratic Club; Richmond County Democratic Club; Nettie Carter-Jackson Democratic Club. She was a lifetime member of the NAACP. Inspired by her love of history, she also dedicated herself to the Association for the Study of Afro-American Life and History, South Jersey Branch, a chapter of the famous organization founded by historian Carter G. Woodson, the originator of the national black history observance, held annually in February.

For her fine contributions, Laura received many awards and citations. The local and national divisions of NANM presented her with awards in 1983 and 1984, respectively. Other awards were given her by the Greengrove Baptist Church's Usher Board, the Archway Day Care Center, the Black Business and Professional Women of Camden and Vicinity, and ASALH, South Jersey Branch. A short recap of her life was published in Dr. Rebecca Batts Butler's *Portraits of Black Role Models in the History of Southern New Jersey*, Acme Craftsmen Publishers, 1985. Still active at the time of her death, Laura died in June of 1994, in Berlin.

PAYNE, J[OHN] CHRISTOPHER, "CHRIS" (1930–1994), pianist, organist, choir director, music teacher, accompanist. The youngest of five sons, Chris was born in Swedesboro, New Jersey, on September 1, 1930 to James A. and Rosa E. (Taylor) Payne, Sr. His father was a native of Essex County, Virginia. After visiting a brother, he migrated to Swedesboro during World War I. Earning a living first as a sharecropper, then as a farm owner, Chris's father sold produce at the town's market on Dock Street, situated along Raccoon Creek. The cargo was loaded onto barges and boats, then transported to Philadelphia, Pennsylvania and Baltimore, Maryland. A native of Hanover, Virginia, Chris's mother moved to Swedesboro to live with a cousin in the early 1920's. His parents met and were married shortly after her arrival. The Paynes worshipped at the First Baptist Church in Swedesboro, where his father served as a deacon. As a result of his parent's deep convictions, Chris and his brothers were raised with a strict religious upbringing. When he was twelve, his father died suddenly. After that time, Chris's eldest brothers, James Jr., Thomas, and Henry, managed the farm and supported the family, while his brother Randolph and he continued with their schooling.

Along with his siblings, Chris was educated in the public schools. Leased by the Swedesboro Board of Education, his all-black grammar school was in the hall that belonged to the Prince Hall Masons, Mt. Lebanon Lodge Number Forty-Seven. Due to the area's large tenant farm population, each classroom contained three grades with a total of fifty to sixty students. Like the majority of the students, Chris did his farm chores before arriving at school each day. Completing his secondary education in integrated classes, he attended Swedesboro Junior High School, and graduated from Swedesboro High School in 1948.

Before he was school age, Chris displayed a marked interest in music, encouraged by his mother. After purchasing a player piano, she had each of her sons watch as she took lessons. Her teacher, Mrs. Johnson, was the organist-choir director at their church and former organist of the Kaighn Avenue Baptist Church, an historic church in Camden City. At the age of four, Chris began to finger the keys of the piano as it played a tune and was soon able to play by ear. Seeing his fascination, his mother started instructing him at age five. Because of his quick progress, Chris came briefly under the tutelage of Mrs. Johnson, then his pastor's wife, Helen Tunstall, who played the pump organ. Through this largely informal training, and his innate talent, Chris learned to play hymns and other simple selections. Because he was also interested in singing, he joined both of the children's choirs at First Baptist.

When he was eleven, Chris played for one year as the organist-choir director of his church. Although very young, he capably performed his duties. The following year, he became the pianist of the Morning Star Baptist Church in Woodstown, whose pastor was the Reverend C. R. Overby. At the suggestion of Overby, who recognized his potential, Chris's mother provided him with his first formal music lessons. Traveling to Williamstown, he began to study the piano with Mr. Edwards of the Edwards School of Music. While engaged in his lessons, he received his first instruction in basic theory and learned to read music. Subsequently, Chris studied with Ethel Hill, a teacher in Swedesboro. Although he played jazz under her tutelage, he abandoned that pursuit and dedicated himself to the performance of sacred and classical music. After Morning Star Baptist Church installed a Kilgen pipe organ, Chris studied with Otto Doran, the organist at Mt. Zion Church in Salem, the main city in Salem County. Later, he took advanced training on the organ with Kenneth Goodman at the Settlement Music School in Philadelphia.

During his teen years, Chris gained significant public exposure as an instrumentalist and a vocalist that fostered his musical development. His high school music teacher, Maryann Gettzinger, presented him in several organ recitals at her church, the Bethesda Methodist Church, and in churches in Atlantic City. Whenever he sang in concerts and plays at school, Chris, who had an exceptional voice, attracted large audiences. His vocal skill earned him membership in the Woodbury Choral Society, a very distinguished group under the direction of S. Edward Davis. However, after developing serious throat problems, he devoted his time to instrumental pursuits.

While playing for a funeral in Swedesboro, Chris attracted the attention of Gretchen Branche Waples, who was greatly impressed by his talent. Besides working with her husband as an undertaker, she was a noted coloratura soprano and the director of the junior choir at the Kaighn Avenue Baptist Church in Camden. Because of the impending retirement of their organist, James Marshall Wheeler, Waples immediately recruited Chris to serve as his replacement, vouching for his qualifications with the church's trustees. In 1949, to gain additional experience and training from Wheeler prior to his departure, Chris finished his tenure at Morningstar Baptist Church, after serving nine years, and started to play at Kaighn Avenue Baptist. Because it was New Jersey's first black Baptist church, organized in 1856 as an outgrowth of summer camp meetings dating back to the year 1838, with a large, active congregation, this was a very prestigious appointment for him.

Within a short time, Chris took a brief leave of absence from Kaighn Avenue Baptist Church to enlist in the U.S. Army. During his absence, Juanita Fernandez, another fine young musician, substituted for him. Following the completion of his basic training at Fort Lee, Virginia, Chris was stationed in military bases in South Carolina and in the southwestern United States. While working as the chaplain's assistant, Chris became the base organist and the founder and director of two choral groups. As a result of his fine work, he received a commendation from the base commander.

When he returned to Camden in 1951, Chris resumed playing for Kaighn Avenue Baptist Church as the full-time organist. At that time, Phillip Johnson directed the senior choir. After Johnson's death, Chris became the organist-choir director. Through the years with its thriving music program, the church had several ensembles: Senior Choir; Chapel Choir; Mass Choir; Women's Choir; Men's Choir; Gospel Chorus; Junior Choir. In the latter part of his forty-four year tenure, Chris served as the minister of music, with the responsibility of maintaining the diverse presentation of music at the church. While he directed the Senior Choir and accompanied the Chapel Choir, assistant directors and accompanists worked with the others, among them: Beatrice Jackson; Mary (Edmonds) Burrell; Rochelle Jackson; Gretchen Waples; Teddy Johnson. With the Senior Choir, Chris presented special concerts of sacred classical music. He and the choir also traveled extensively with the church pastors, throughout the region and to New York, Ohio, and several southern states. Periodically, Chris coached students individually, and in group classes at the church. In conjunction with his duties, he was a member of the Hampton University Choir Directors and Organists Guild, and regularly attended the Hampton University Ministers' Conference and Annual Choir Directors and Organists Guild Workshop, that met annually at Hampton University in Virginia during the month of June.

As an outgrowth of his own endeavors, Chris presented annual joint concerts, featuring the performance of classical music and Negro spirituals, with his close musical associates. He collaborated on many of these programs with Allen Foster, Sr., a former member of Kaighn Avenue Baptist Church who was the organist-choir director of Pinn Memorial Baptist Church in Philadelphia. Besides performing alternately at each other's church, they performed for many other congregations in southern New Jersey and Philadelphia. Another peer with whom Chris presented concerts was Wayne Triplett, who was an equally accomplished church musician in southern New Jersey.

Chris's outstanding reputation brought him many requests to perform in the community. For several years, he played for the Camden Salvation Army's annual holiday banquet, and other similar affairs. Most notably, while employed as the supervisor of the maintenance department at the John Wanamaker's store in Philadelphia, Chris was privileged to play the famous Wanamaker organ, the largest pipe organ in the world, each day during his lunch break.

Subsequent to his retirement from John Wanamaker's, Chris worked for the Teledyne Company for nearly fifteen years. Throughout his career, his dedication and distinctive style was lauded by his musical peers and audiences alike. His commendations included citations from the mayor of Swedesboro, among others. At Kaighn Avenue Baptist Church, he was specially honored on his thirtieth and forty-second anniversaries as the church organist. In December of 1994, Chris died from the complications of diabetes. As a final tribute, Kaighn Avenue Baptist Church dedicated its organ to his memory in 1995.

PUGGSLEY, [INEZ] CARLINE LEWIS (1896–1983), pianist, music teacher, social worker, YWCA administrator. The daughter of T. F. and Mary "Mollie" (née ?) Carter, Carline was born in Marianna, Arkansas in May of 1896. Her father, who was a school teacher and native of Mississippi, died when she was very young. After his death, Carline's mother, who was a native of Tennessee, married James Turner. Thereupon, Carline and her older brother, Olden, were raised on her step-father's farm in Independence Township (in this period, Marianna was incorporated within the township).

Educated in Little Rock, Carline received her high school diploma and college degree from Philander Smith College. After completing her education, she began her career as a school teacher in Marianna, teaching junior high and high school. In the early 1920's, she met and married Granville R. Lewis, Sr., who was a dentist. Their only child, Granville Jr., became a dentist as well.

In the early 1930's, Carline and her family moved to Little Rock. Although she initially pursued teaching, she soon developed a serious interest in social work. Consequently, she entered Fisk University in Nashville, Tennessee to obtain a degree in sociology. After completion of her studies, Carline obtained a position as the director of the Phillis Wheatley Branch of the Greater Little Rock YWCA, which she held from 1937 until 1942. Upon leaving the YWCA, she worked as the director of the Little Rock area's USO (United Services Organization), providing for the needs of military personnel in the service during World War II. In 1944, after her husband's death, Carline traveled to Calcutta, India to serve as the USO Club Director of the Burma-India Area. When she returned to the United States in 1946, she accepted a position as the executive director of the Frances Harper YWCA, a segregated facility, in Camden, New Jersey, later that same year.

Despite the demands of her administrative duties at the Frances Harper YWCA, Carline, who was a prominent resident of Camden, substantially engaged in teaching music as an avocation, from the early 1950's until her death. Enthralled with music from childhood, she studied piano with private teachers in Arkansas throughout her early schooling. Since her musical gifts were considerable, she was inspired to further study as an adult. Living briefly in Ohio and Illinois during unspecified periods in the 1920's and 1930's, Carline pursued advanced music studies at Oberlin College and at the Chicago Conservatory of Music, respectively.

In 1947, Carline married Louis E. Puggsley, who was an eminent flutist, conductor, and member of the black symphony orchestras that were prevalent in Camden and Philadelphia from the early to mid 1900's. Their mutual love of music engendered the establishment of a large music studio, with five pianos, in their home. With both accepting numerous pupils, Carline taught piano and Louis taught flute. Her effectiveness as a teacher soon advanced her reputation within the community. For nearly thirty years, she mentored her students by presenting them in recitals at local churches and at the YWCA. Under her tutelage, several of Carline's students gained entry into noted schools of music: Settlement School of Music in Philadelphia, Pennsylvania; Esther Boyer School of Music at Temple University, also in Philadelphia; the Westminster Choir College of Princeton University in Princeton, New Jersey; the School of Music at Howard University in Washington, D.C. She was equally influen-

124

tial in the musical education of her grandchildren, of whom Dr. Carol Lewis, notably, became an exceptional professional musician, composer, director, and music teacher in southern New Jersey. Although a skillful musician herself, Carline performed on rare occassion.

During her tenure at the Frances Harper YWCA, Carline managed the controversial merger, and consequential racial integration, of the agency with the Stevens Street YWCA, in Camden. An active church member, when she first moved to the city she joined the Ferry Avenue Methodist (later UM) Church. Later, she became a member of another Camden church, the Parkside UM Church. She was a member of the Zeta Phi Beta Sorority, the NAACP, and a member of the board of directors of the Mary H. Thomas Nursery in Camden.

A widow since 1967, Carline died on December 9, 1983, at the age of eighty-seven. The music for her funeral service, held at the Parkside UM Church on December 14, was performed by members of the Philadelphia Philharmonic Orchestra.

RICHARDSON, IONA DAVIS (b. 1927), pianist, organist, choir director, music teacher, accompanist. The daughter of Joseph Henry and Ledoshia (Henderson) Davis, Iona was born in Camden on January 25, 1927. Her father, who was born in Camden in 1889, was employed as the custodian of the Powell School for forty years. Born in 1890, her mother was a native of Elizabeth City, North Carolina and was educated at the Roanoake Institute. When Iona's parents met, her father was a widower with six children. After marrying, they had four offspring. Iona was ninth of the ten Davis progeny: Joseph Henry Jr., John, Percy, Eleanor, Evelyn, Robert, Glynne Alveria, Dallas Lee, Iona, and Burem Randolph.

Educated in the public schools of Camden, Iona received her early instruction at the segregated Powell School. Because her teachers and principals were considerable influences in her life, she remembered each of them: Lenore Madden Ash, May Saunders Moore, Marguerite Jordan Carter, Catherine Palmer Johnson, Lillian C. Reynolds, Rebecca Batts Butler, Robert Loving, and Mensfield Fitting. Singing and playing a variety of music daily, including hymns and spirituals, nurtured her intense passion for music. Exhibiting a great musical aptitude at age six, Iona enjoyed touching the keys of the school's piano and singing each note's four part harmony. During her schooling, she was also impressed by the lessons in black history. Because of her rich experiences, she was a devoted student.

Singing in Sunday school likewise fostered Iona's propensity for music. By the time she was eight, Iona's parents were given a piano by the organist of Camden's Mt. Hope UAME Church, where they worshipped. Eager to play, she was self-taught for a few years. Iona's first formal music instruction was at age twelve, under the tutelage of James Marshall Wheeler, who was a very fine and steadfast teacher. After he was drafted into the Army, he sent his pupils to study with Emily Lucken Brown, who was an equally capable teacher. The wonderful rapport that Brown established with her caused Iona to flourish; well-placed compliments especially built her self-confidence. Achieving a wonderful touch on the piano, Iona soon started to accompany her older sister Glynne, a fabulous lyric soprano who eventually joined the chorus of the Dra Mu Opera Company of Philadelphia. The ensemble was founded by Raymond Lowden Smith, a noted African American musician and conductor, to give black vocalists the opportunity to perform in serious works of opera. Challenged by her sister's vocal expertise, Iona mastered a difficult repertoire of classical music.

In 1941, Iona entered the integrated Clara S. Burroughs Junior High School. In September of the following year, she was one of the first twelve black students who were transferred to the academic program at Woodrow Wilson High School. From the time of her enrollment, Iona was thoroughly disheartened by experiences in the school. In contrast to her early education, she and her classmates were discouraged or barred from pursuing their academic and extra-curricular interests. Despite Iona's great capacity for music, she was unable to join the Glee Club or play the school's pipe organ. During this same period, she was further affected by seeing her sister stand behind the stage scenery at Camden High School and sing solos from *Naughty Marietta*, while a white student performed the role on stage.

As a result of the racism she encountered in secondary school, Iona turned to her church to engage in her musical pursuits. She played the piano for the Sunday School and for special events, such as Tom Thumb weddings. Although Iona had a burning desire to play Mt. Hope's organ, she was forced to wait until age eighteen, when, in realization of her dream, she was appointed organist-choir director.

Under the tutelage of her pastor, Reverend M. R. Spencer, and Bishop Walters, a bishop of the Christian Methodist Episcopal denomination, Iona studied the Methodist Episcopal liturgical calendar, learning to select appropriate hymns, and liturgical colors for the stoles of their choir vestments. During the first years of her tenure, she also took two years of advanced music studies. At age nineteen, she was instructed by Robert Haley, a music teacher at Camden High School who taught privately in his own studio on Market Street. When she was nineteen, Iona traveled to Palmyra to study theory with Myrtle Van Buren Watson. Watson, who achieved prominence as a pianist, teacher, and accompanist, was the wife of Reverend William Watson, a UAME minister and noted baritone soloist. Myrtle and William Watson had also been members of the Dra Mu Opera Company in Philadelphia, she as assistant pianist and vocalist, he singing lead roles and in the chorus.

Exuberant in personality and her work, Iona served in an exceptional fashion. At Mt. Hope, she directed four choirs, with singers from age five through adult. At special holiday services, Iona routinely featured prominent local soloists, among who were Walter Shelton, James Burch, and her sister Glynne. (Significantly, her musically talented family includes her niece, Osceola Davis, a celebrated opera diva who performed world-wide.) For many of these occasions, Iona presented her original compositions, such as *Thou Art My God*. Traveling extensively throughout the UAME conference, she presented her choirs in one concert each month, in Newark and other large cities. She also performed in fellowship with local congregations: Harris Temple AMEZ Church and Kaighn Avenue Baptist Church in Camden; Asbury Methodist Church in Pennsauken.

A hallmark of Iona's directing was teaching her members to sing *a capella,* a challenging task, with a repertoire favoring spirituals. Her assessment of her Intermediate Choir's magnificent *a capella* performance before a large audience attending a UAME conference at

Yale University in New Haven, Connecticut, indicates how proud she was of their achievement: "It was superb, the highlight of my life." This feat also brought her numerous plaudits for outstanding choral direction. For twenty-five years, Iona also presented joint concerts with J. Albert Bray, the organist-choir director of the Chestnut Street UAME Church in Camden, using seventy voice choirs.

When Mt. Hope UAME moved into the Parkside section of Camden in the early 1970's, Iona was thrilled to have the use of an American pipe organ, that she called "an instrument unto God." After devoting herself to its mastery, she attained an even higher level of inspiration and skill in her work.

In 1968, Iona performed another memorable deed in her career as a musician, as a result of her employment as a Human Relations Coordinator at RCA in Camden. On behalf of the company, she played in Atlanta during the funeral of the slain civil rights leader, Dr. Martin Luther King, Jr. Participating in this unforgettable national event was deeply moving to her.

Devoting a considerable amount of time to teaching piano and voice, Iona instructed her young pupils at Mt. Hope, and her adult students in her home. Because she was denied the use of the organ as a youngster, she provided her pupils with early opportunities to play the instrument at the church. As a rule, she quickly advanced her students through the fundamentals, encouraging their progress with reinforcement from their parents. Iona also mentored students by presenting them in recitals. Two of her charges, continuing with their studies, obtained positions playing for the First Baptist Church in Jericho, New Jersey and Nazarene Baptist Church in Camden.

In 1988 after serving for more than fifty years, Iona retired as the organist-choir director of Mt. Hope, especially to allow younger musicians the opportunity to pursue careers in the church. Married since 1945, she and her husband, Thomas Richardson, Sr., are the parent's of two children: Wanna Eugenia and Thomas Jr. Iona is currently a resident of Palm Beach, Florida.

VOORHEES, ESSIE HOLMES (b. 1929), pianist, organist, choir director, music teacher, accompanist, health and human services worker. Born to William Cleveland and Roberta (Jones) Holmes in Camden in 1929, Essie was the ninth of fifteen children. Her parents, who were very religious, met and married in Camden. At the time, her father, who was a native of the city, was a deacon at Baptist Temple Church; her mother, who was born in Philadelphia and raised in Newark, served as its pianist. In emulation of their mother, three of Essie's gifted siblings also taught music or played for churches: William; Helen; Mae. Educated in the Camden public schools, Essie attended grammar school at the Powers Public School and the John Greenleaf Whittier Public School. She completed her secondary education at the Cooper B. Hatch Junior High School and Camden High School.

Raised by her mother's dictum, "Music is your life," it was Essie's principal pastime from early childhood. When she was school age, her mother, who was a dynamic musician and music teacher, taught her to sing and play the piano. After learning the fundamentals, she began to play in programs at school, to the delight of her teachers. While attending the Whittier School, Essie took intermediate instruction on the piano under the tutelage of Sadye Gibson Taylor, another prominent local music teacher and choir member at Macedonia AME Church in Camden.

Working in her mother's music retail store, the Universal Music Store, Essie performed newly released gospel music for customers, and assisted with preparing merchandise for sale. This unique experience fostered her growth immeasurably. At Baptist Temple Church, Essie and seven of her brothers and sisters also constituted a large portion of the choir. As a result of their animated performances, engendered by their mother's spirited playing, her entire family gained a fine reputation for its musical prowess.

Because of her own ample talent and advantageous training, Essie was soon provided with beneficial opportunities to engage in her musical pursuits. At the age of twelve, she was hired to play at Harris Temple AMEZ Church, for the sum of one dollar per service. For three or four years, she performed her duties very capably. At Camden High School, she attracted the attention of her music teacher, who encouraged her talents by having her play for various activities. When she was eighteen, she gained additional public exposure as the accompanist of a vocal group that performed throughout the city.

Thereafter, Essie obtained several appointments at churches in Camden City and the region. Because of her great versatility and boundless energy, she oftentimes served two or three churches simultaneously, in coordination with a musical associate. Early in her career, Essie continued her studies under the tutelage of James Marshall Wheeler, then Jesse I. Hamilton, Sr., both who were renowned for their expertise. Later, she took lessons at the Don Christ Studios and at the Merchantville Conservatory of Music. This advanced training broadened her employment opportunities. Among the Camden churches that Essie worked for were Scott's AUMP (later Methodist) Church, Holy Trinity Baptist, Refuge Baptist, Canaan Baptist, New Jerusalem Baptist, Broadway UM Church, Victory Temple Baptist, Faith Baptist, and Woodland Presbyterian. Besides serving White Oak Baptist Church in Lindenwold, she also played in Newark and Philadelphia.

For Essie, teaching music was a natural outgrowth of working with her mother. In the mid 1950's, she moved to Newark to help her mother teach for a few years. At that time, Essie's mother, who had established a large store and music studio on Raymond Boulevard and Locke Street, had an enormous enrollment of students. Two of Essie's sisters, Pearl and Mae, also worked in the studio. Returning to Camden by the late 1950's, Essie offered private lessons in her home. From the early 1960's, she consistently presented her pupils in recitals. Besides using the churches for her programs, she worked in community centers, such as the Camden YWCA, the West Atco Improvement League, and the Neighborhood Center of Camden.

An accomplished accompanist, Essie devoted a significant portion of her time to promoting vocalists in concert, and working with choral groups. Most often, she accompanied one of her mother's former students, Carrie Langford Collier, who achieved national prominence as a gospel artist. In the mid 1980's, after joining the Marian Anderson Music Guild, Camden Chapter of the National

Association of Negro Musicians, Essie performed much of this undertaking on behalf of the organization.

Besides her music career, Essie inherited her mother's keen business sense, and engaged in various entrepeneurial ventures. After graduating from high school on June 19, 1947, she attended the Spriggs and Donaldson School of Beauty Culture in Philadelphia. Earning her diploma in 1950, she completed her requisite apprenticeships and secured her New Jersey and Pennsylvania beautician's licenses and operator's licenses, in 1951 and 1954, respectively. Subsequently, Essie opened her own shops, first at 728 Mt. Vernon Street, then at 552 Walnut Street in Camden.

A very hard-working individual, Essie was later employed in a group home for the mentally retarded, and as a home health aide. Her work in human services motivated her to attend, in the 1980's, Glassboro State College and Rutgers University's Cook College. Completing various courses, she earned multiple certifications from state agencies and the schools: New Jersey Department of Human Services, Division of Mental Retardation; New Jersey Department of Health; Rutgers Coop Extension, Home Economic Division. Upon completing her training, she operated a boarding home for young men who were mentally retarded.

Married in the late 1950's, Essie and her former husband, Albert Voorhees, are the parents of one daughter, Denise, and two sons, Albert Jr., and Clifford. Her daughter, in particular, is an accomplished musician. Remarkably, Essie also cared for nineteen foster children. Exceedingly dedicated and generous, she has declined to take many awards in her life. Those which Essie did accept include a Governor's Proclamation for Recognition of Outstanding Family Foster Care and a citation from the Marian Anderson Music Guild, Camden Branch of the NANM. Currently retired and a resident of Camden, Essie engages in her musical pursuits on a part-time basis.

WATSON, MYRTLE VAN BUREN (1902–1982), pianist, organist, choir director, music teacher, accompanist, chorister. The youngest of Homer Grant and Katherine S. (née ?) Van Buren's five children, Myrtle was born in New Haven, Connecticut on July 21, 1902. Her parents, natives of New York, were born in 1870 and 1876, respectively. Myrtle's sister Hilda was their only other child to survive infancy. When Myrtle was thirteen, her family settled in Philadelphia, Pennsylvania. Educated in the public schools, she graduated from the Philadelphia High School for Girls, a select school in the district. Faithful church members, the Van Burens attended Allen AME Church, located at Seventeenth and Bainbridge. Her father, who worked as a porter in New Haven, earned a living in Philadelphia as a foreman at an ice cream manufacturing company.

A precocious musical talent, Myrtle began study of the piano just before her fifth birthday, and performed publicly at age six and a half years old. Because of her remarkable skill, she was given private instruction by a Professor Fowler, who taught at the Yale University Conservatory of Music. Through his instruction, she mastered her fundamental skills. At age ten, Myrtle was invited to perform with a distinguished all-black symphony orchestra in New Haven, a feat that fostered her musical growth and brought her glowing praise from many admirers. Prior to her family leaving Connecticut, she enrolled in classes at the Yale conservatory for further preparation.

By the time she was a teenager and living in Philadelphia, Myrtle, who was well-versed in many types of music, was recognized in the community for her singular accomplishments. During high school, she started to teach piano to young children. Her skill as a performer was manifest in programs at school, and recitals at several churches. Also endowed with a fine mezzo-soprano voice, Myrtle was a noted member of the choir at Allen AME. At the time, its music program was directed by Francis A. Clark, an eminent musician, composer, and arranger. Significantly, he had collaborated on several hymns with Reverend Charles Albert Tindley, one of gospel music's creators.

While singing at Allen AME, Myrtle became acquainted with a fellow chorister, William L. Watson. A marvelous tenor oftentimes featured as a soloist, he was studying under the tutelage of Henry Gurney, a tenor with international fame as a concert artist. William, who was born in a log cabin in Clayton, Alabama, had first moved to Philadelphia at age eighteen. Myrtle and he later married and had one daughter, Myrtle Helen, whom they called "little Myrtle."

Upon her decision to engage in music as a profession, Myrtle began working as a church musician in the early to mid 1920's. Her most notable position as an organist-choir director, that she started in the late 1920's and held for sixteen years, was at Zoar Methodist Church. Prior to her work there, Myrtle had joined the choir at St. Thomas' Episcopal Church, the nation's first black Episcopal parish, founded July 17, 1794 by Absalom Jones (also called the African Church of St. Thomas.) Along with Mother Bethel AME Church, organized July 29, 1794, it was an outgrowth of the Free African Society established by Jones and Richard Allen in 1787.

During the Depression, Myrtle secured work teaching music in community centers, through the Music Project of the federal government's Works Progress Administration. To augment her qualifications as a professional, she took courses at Temple University and the University of Pennsylvania. Since she had a serious interest in vocal music, Myrtle also took private lessons for nine years with her husband's teacher, Henry Gurney. In the 1930's and 1940's, she and William conducted their Watson Studio, at 1405 North Twelfth Street and 654 North Thirteenth Street. While he taught voice, Myrtle taught piano, voice, theory, ear training, and sight reading. Besides promoting their students in recitals and concerts, Myrtle presented her husband in a series of concerts at churches and large performance halls, such as Town Hall, at Broad and Race Streets. She later included their daughter, who was a flutist, on several occasions. As a volunteer during the 1940's, Myrtle served as accompanist for the choral ensembles at the Western Community House, a Quaker social service institution in the city, at 1613 South Street.

In the mid 1940's, Myrtle and William joined the prestigious Dra Mu Opera Company, founded by Raymond Lowden Smith to promote the performance of grand opera by black artists in Philadelphia. Smith, a noted conductor of another all-black ensemble, the E. Gilbert Anderson Memorial Symphony Orchestra, later renamed the Philadelphia Concert Orchestra, was its general manager. He engaged prominent white artists, including Henri Elkan, who served as conductor, to stage the company's highly successful annual productions between 1946 and 1954: *La traviata, Pagliacci* [sic]; *Cavalleria rusticana; Carmen; Hansel and Gretel; Faust; Aïda.* For nearly four years, Myrtle was the ensemble's assistant pianist, as well as a member of the chorus. During the 1947–1948 season, she was featured as the pianist for the ballet, choreographed by dance master Thomas Cannon, in their production of *Carmen.* Besides singing in the chorus, her husband sang the role of Canio in the 1946 staging of *Pagliacci.* Their daughter danced in Dra Mu's corps de ballet.

During the latter part of Myrtle's productive career as a musician, she resided and conducted her work in southern New Jersey. This move was effected by her husband's desire to enter the ministry. He first earned a bachelor of sacred theology degree from Miller University in the 1950's (and later was awarded an honorary doctorate). After joining the UAME denomination in 1959, his ordination as a deacon and elder resulted in the family's relocation. Serving the New Jersey conference, he was assigned pastor of three churches: St. Mark UAME, Glassboro; St. Paul UAME Church, Palmyra; Spencer UAME, Woodstown. While fulfilling her duties as a minister's wife, Myrtle served as organist-choir director and minister of music at her husband's charges. Because of her masterful direction, her choir's excelled in performances throughout the area, especially in Palmyra, Camden, Woodstown, and at annual UAME conference meetings.

Apart from her church work, Myrtle maintained her full agenda of musical activities in the community. She taught piano, voice, and theory, sponsored her numerous students in recitals, and performed as a concert artist and accompanist until late in life. As a life time member of the National Association of Negro Musicians, Myrtle promoted its mission, especially the performance of classical and sacred music written by African American composers.

As a consequence of her dedication and achievements as a musician, Myrtle was highly respected and acclaimed by the community, her church, and her musical peers. She died in Woodstown in August of 1982, at the age of eighty, and is interred in the cemetery of Spencer UAME Church.

WHEELER, JAMES MARSHALL (1911–1979), pianist, organist, choir director, music teacher, accompanist, conductor. Born in Dela-

134

ware on July 1, 1911, James was the only child of Warren and Flora L. (née ?) Wheeler. By the time he was school age his parents moved to Camden, New Jersey. Receiving his early education in the Camden public schools, he attended the John Greenleaf Whittier Public School and the Cooper B. Hatch. Junior High School. Completing his secondary education in Philadelphia, James graduated with a degree in mathematics from Central High School, the elite public boys' school.

James was first instructed in music by his mother, a gifted pianist herself. In his early lessons, he displayed a brilliance indicative of his laudable future. At thirteen, he studied pipe organ with the organist of the prestigious Kaighn Avenue Baptist Church in Camden. New Jersey's first black Baptist congregation, and the outgrowth of summer camp meetings dating back to 1838, it was organized in 1856, in Kaighnsville, the city's first African American settlement. After a few months, James continued his organ lessons as the student of W. Franklin Hoxter, Sr. A famed Philadelphia musician, he routinely taught and performed in New Jersey. Within that time because of his rapid progress, James was appointed assistant organist of his church, the Chestnut Street UAME Church in Camden. Then, in 1929, he became the organist of Kaighn Avenue Baptist Church.

Graduating from high school that same year, James, intent on a career as a musician and music teacher, enrolled in the Philadelphia Academy for the Arts, as an organ major. He received two bachelor of arts degrees from the school, one in music and the other in music education, and took graduate courses in theory. In the spring of 1935, James studied at the Furhman School of Music in Camden, with Clarence Furhman. Later, he obtained other academic training at Rutgers University, in New Jersey, and in two Philadelphia institutions: Temple University, and the University of Pennsylvania.

In 1936, the federal government's Works Progress Administration, established in Camden the previous fall, afforded James an excellent opportunity to apply his craft. Respected both by his teachers and peers, he was offered a job in the WPA Federal Music Project for Camden County. Since the supervisor of the county project was Joseph Furhman, of the Furhman Music School, James's prior enrollment there proved advantageous in securing this position. Assigned

135

to work at the Hunton Branch YMCA, a segregated "Y" located at 1300 South Sixth Street in Camden, James became the second director of its Hunton Branch WPA Band, comprised of eleven members of the Hunton Branch Symphony Orchestra, the all-black ensemble founded at the facility in 1921. Eldon Raynor, a prominent resident in the city who was a charter member and conductor of the orchestra, preceded him as the band's first director. Eventually conducting both ensembles, James's success enhanced his community standing.

From the mid 1930's until his retirement, James taught music in his own studio, and in the public schools of Camden. Because of his expertise, he was sought after as a private instructor by several of the city's most talented students. His great influence was evident, as many of them became dedicated musicians and teachers; a few examples are Theodore H. Brooks, Jesse I. Hamilton, Jr., Juanita Fernandez, Audrey Canois Givens, J. Christopher Payne, Iona Davis Richardson, and Ellen Blair. James's initial teaching position in the school district was at the Cooper B. Hatch Junior High School. However, he was best known for his nearly forty year tenure as a music teacher at the Pyne Poynt Middle School. The first black teacher to obtain employment at the school, he was eventually promoted as head of its music department. Both popular and effective, he devoted himself to inspiring his student's talents and appreciation for music.

Drafted into the military during World War II, James served in the south Pacific as a member of the 93rd Division, U.S. Army. During his absence, Emily Lucken Brown substituted for him at Kaighn Avenue Baptist Church and trained many of his students. After his return, he resumed playing for Kaighn Avenue Baptist for a few years, then retired in 1951, having served twenty-two years. That same year, James became the organist of Wesley AMEZ Church, working with Rose Payne Wilson, the choir director. However, with his health in decline, he resigned from Wesley in 1955. Between the late 1950's and the mid 1960's, James served as the organist-choir director of two Philadelphia churches: Mt. Olive Holy Temple, a member church of the Mt. Sinai Holiness Church, Inc.; Mt. Pisgah AME Church. During this period he was treated for kidney failure.

Despite his serious health problems, James dedicated himself to his beloved pursuits in music and education for almost fifteen more years. When family and friends expressed their concern, he told them: "Music is my life." Because of his statewide reputation, he was elected

James Marshall Wheeler, one of Camden's most respected, and influential musicians and teachers, pictured in the 1970's. Courtesy of Jesse I. Hamilton, Jr.

to the board of directors of the Westminster Choir College of Princeton University, in Princeton. In 1968, James became the organist-choir director of St. Augustine's Episcopal Church in Camden, which proved to be his last position. Sometime in his ninth year of service, he was diagnosed with leukemia. The news of his illness inspired Lois K. Harris, his successor at the Wesley AMEZ Church, to recruit their peers to perform a benefit concert on his behalf. This effort resulted in the creation of the Ecumenical Choir of Camden, New Jersey & Vicinity, and, out of respect for James's wishes, the James Marshall Wheeler Scholarship Fund, for the benefit of undergraduate students who were majoring in music. In the debut concert at Camden High School on September 10, 1968, the choir extolled his phenomenal life's work in a program that featured presentations by former members of the Hunton Branch WPA band, and his numerous music students. The choir continued this effort in annual concerts for four years, awarding scholarships to a few students.

As his illness progressed, James resigned from his work and his pastimes, including serving as the Commander of the Clarence Hill Post, number 1297, Veterans of Foreign Wars. He was also a gold card member of the Pride of Camden Elks, Lodge number eighty-three. Succumbing to the effects of the leukemia, James died in Camden on November 4, 1979. His funeral service was held at Chestnut Street UAME Church on November 8. A photo and brief sketch of his life is published in two books by Dr. Rebecca Batts Butler: *Profiles of outstanding Blacks in South Jersey during the 1950's, 1960's, 1970's,* Reynolds Publishers, 1980; *Portraits of Black Role Models in the History of Southern New Jersey,* Acme Craftsmen Publishers, 1985.

WILSON, ROSANNA "ROSE" PAYNE (1888–1989), vocalist, choir director, music teacher, pianist. Born in Camden, New Jersey on November 2, 1888, Rose was the daughter of John H. and Sarah C. (Townsend) Payne. Her parents were enslaved during the early part of their lives. John H. Payne, the son of Thaddeus Payne and an unknown mother, was born on December 25, 1832 in Virginia. For many years, he earned a living as a sailor. When he retired from work at sea, he became a day laborer. The daughter of James and Rosanna (Hall) Townsend, who were born in 1819 and 1818, respectively, Rose's mother was born in Delaware on September 29, 1845. She worked as a domestic. Meeting after they each moved to Camden, John and Sarah were married in the city at 918 Mt. Vernon Street, Sarah's place of residence, on January 15, 1885. Their ceremony was performed by the Reverend Abram Anderson, the pastor of Wesley AMEZ Church. The church, founded in 1844 at Ann and Sycamore

Street, was a leading institution in the community. Because of Sarah's role as a mother of the church, an honor she earned by carrying bricks in her apron when Wesley built its first brick structure in 1880, each generation of the Payne family remained faithful members. Rose had three siblings: Joseph H. Payne, born June 12, 1886; William T. Townsend, a half-brother, born May 12, 1870; a second half-sibling who died in infancy or childhood. Another relative, Gladys Estella Payne, born March 4, 1906, was also a member of their household.

From the time she was a small child, Rose's father entertained her and her family with fascinating stories of his voyages and gave them exotic presents that he had obtained in foreign ports. She delighted in recounting these dramatic, and sometimes hair raising tales to her friends. Likewise treasuring the gifts from her father, Rose kept many until her death.

Upon reaching school-age, Rose attended the Mt. Vernon Public School, a segregated grammar school in Camden. Later in her life, she furthered her education by enrolling in adult evening classes in that same district.

Rose was first exposed to music, learning to sing hymns and spirituals, while worshipping with her family at Wesley AMEZ Church. Because of her inherent ability and love for music, her parents gave her piano and voice lessons with private teachers as a child. As a teenager, Rose was encouraged to use her talent at church. Consequently at age fifteen, she founded and directed a Sunday school choir. Using this group as a core, she then created a larger ensemble with singers from other churches, and recruited her schoolmate, Theodora Hayes (later Allison), who was an exceedingly gifted pianist, to serve as its accompanist. Under Rose's capable direction, they were well-received in city-wide performances.

At age twenty-three, Rose married John A. Wilson. Born in New Jersey in 1879, at that time he was a resident of Norristown, Pennsylvania. Their wedding ceremony, performed by the Reverend I. B. Walters, took place in her parents' home at 717 South 8th Street in Camden, on June 22, 1912. Rose and John lived with her parents for several years, then moved into their own home. The couple had no children. After John's death in the early 1940's, Rose did not re-marry.

When she was twenty-nine, Rose joined the People's Choral Society of Philadelphia, Pennsylvania,at the recommendation of violinist Edwin Francis Hill. One of an illustrious family of musicians,

Rose Payne Wilson, a beautiful contralto, directed choirs at Wesley AMEZ Church in Camden for more than fifty years. Photo, circa 1910, courtesy of Niramay Smith

he was serving as the choir director of Macedonia AME Church in Camden. The society, under the direction of his brother, Alfred J. Hill, was a prestigious ensemble founded in 1908 by Azalia Hackley, the renowned African American soprano. In later years, Rose often proudly repeated to family and associates Edwin Hill's introduction of her to his brother: "I have brought you something good out of
140

Camden." A gifted contralto, she sang with the society from 1917 until 1925. Traveling by ferry, Rose attended the rehearsals that were held at the First African Presbyterian Church. Besides performing locally, the society gave concerts in cities along the eastern seaboard. Sharing the stage with the People's Choral Society during its performances were elite and lesser known artists of the concert world, among them R. Nathaniel Dett, Roland Hayes, Viola Hill, and Marian Anderson. Notably in the late 1910's and early 1920's, the society performed benefit concerts for Anderson, who at that time was an aspirant to the concert stage. In February of 1919, Rose herself sponsored an appearance of the group at her church.

Simultaneous to singing with the People's Choral Society, Rose joined the Alfred J. Hill Voice Culture Class. With Hill and Agnes Reifsnyder, a prominent white music teacher, as the director and instructor, respectively, the class had highly talented concert artists, including Marian Anderson, Viola Hill, Walter Nicholson, Rose Maiden, and Helen Milton, and elocutionists Irving Underhill and Helen Underhill. Performing principally in churches and in music halls in Philadelphia, Hill presented the singers in demonstrations of vocal technique, recitals, and concerts. Top pianists, W. Russell Johnson and others, served as accompanists. Along with her classmates' work, Rose's featured solos were favorably noted in press reviews. After completing her studies with Hill, she performed in Camden as a soloist for more than thirty years, in concerts sponsored by churches, and community organizations, such as the Hunton Branch YMCA.

With her heightened store of knowledge, Rose was very effective in training her Sunday school choir. Later, that same proficiency allowed her to become the director of Wesley's Senior Choir. During her fifty year tenure serving in this capacity, Rose worked with a series of outstanding organists: Arthur Daniels, James R. Allison, Jr., James Marshall Wheeler, and Lois Custis Harris. With these musicians' spirited accompaniment, she and the choir presented a diverse and challenging repertoire of sacred and classical music. As a soloist, Rose further inspired the congregation with her own sublime interpretations of hymns, gospel, anthems, and oratorios.

After her retirement as the choir director of Wesley AMEZ in 1972, Rose, whose devotion to music was extra-ordinary, continued to sing each Sunday and on special occasions. Carried into church on Palm Sunday at the age of ninety-seven, she captivated the attention of all present with her moving rendition of *The Palms*. Held in the highest esteem, Rose was bestowed with innumerable honors by her church and the community.

In the mid 1980's, Rose donated a large part of her personal music collection to the Marian Anderson Music Guild, Camden Chapter of the National Association of Negro Musicians. She entrusted the remainder of her memorabilia with two members of Wesley AMEZ Church: Niramay Smith, who was for many years her physical caretaker; Mrs. Laura Brown, who assisted her with business and legal transactions. Spending her final years living in a convalescent home, Rose died February 15, 1989, in Mt. Laurel, New Jersey, at the age of 100.

WORMACK, MABEL HOPKINS (1902–1988), pianist, organist, choir director, music teacher, accompanist. One of six children, Mabel was born in Camden to Noah and Maggie (Ford) Hopkins on July 9, 1902. Her father, who was a native of Delaware, died when she was a small child. After his death, her mother, a native of Virginia, operated a boarding house and worked as a huckster to support the family. Sometime between 1910 and 1920, her mother married Daniel Mitchel, who helped raise Mabel, her brothers, Noah and Albert Elwood, and her sister Maryetta. (Two other siblings had died in childhood.) Being religious, the family worshipped at the Kaighn Avenue Baptist Church in Camden. Mabel received her formal education in the Camden public schools, attending the Mt. Vernon Public School. Her additional education is unknown. Eventually marrying, her husband was Norman Wormack.

By the time she was school age, Mabel displayed a recognizable talent for music. As a result, her mother provided her with piano lessons at the age of seven. Her first teacher was a member of the Tenth Street Baptist Church in Camden. Within a short time, Mabel's adept playing inspired members of her family, particularly her sister Maryetta, to sing with her. Eager to perform for other people, she

142

began to play for Sunday school exercises at church. Maryetta, reminiscing about Mabel's life, stated: "This led her to participate in many other programs and activities." When she was a teenager, Mabel studied organ at a music conservatory in Philadelphia. After completing her studies, she was hired as one of the school's instructors.

By the early 1920's, Mabel, who was regarded as an expert music teacher, started giving piano lessons privately in her home in Camden. Although the majority of her pupils were children, she also trained adults, particularly later in her life. To foster her students' talents, she presented them in multiple recitals each year, most often at local churches. Still intent in her work during the 1960's and 1970's, Mabel promoted her pupils in the *Amateur Hour*, a monthly showcase and competition for local talent at the Camden YWCA. On occasion, such as Black History Month, she appeared as a guest artist for community programs, presenting the works of noted black composers J. Rosamond Johnson, Hall Johnson, and W. C. Handy, especially for the benefit of young audiences.

As a church musician, Mable's longest tenure was as the pianist-choir director of the Faith Baptist Church in Camden. In her work at Faith Baptist and other churches, she was very effective in training her choirs. Desirous of promoting the love of music, she frequently hosted guest soloists in Sunday afternoon concerts. For several years, Mabel also collaborated with Roberta Jones Holmes, a dynamic Camden church musician and music teacher.

Engaging in her musical pursuits for more than sixty years, Mabel received numerous requests to perform at community events. At the age of eighty-three, she was still playing for funerals, retirement dinners, and similar affairs. For her outstanding accomplishments and dedication, she received awards and commendations, including a certificate of appreciation from the Marian Anderson Music Guild, Camden Branch NANM in 1987.

In 1984, failing health induced Mabel to finally retire. Two years later she moved to Atlantic City to live with her niece, Theda Dittimus. So she could play for her own pleasure, she brought her piano with her. Mabel died April 17, 1988, in Atlantic City, at age 85.

WORTHINGTON, RUTH ROBERTS (b. 1917), pianist, organist, choir director, accompanist, radio broadcast performer. The fifth of thirteen children, Ruth was born in Moorestown, New Jersey to the Reverend Oscar A. and Alice C. (Dixon) Roberts. A native of Boston, Massachusetts, her father was ordained as a minister in the AME Church when she was ten years old. Self-educated and quite industrious, early in his life he had traveled to England with the Salvation Army. Ruth's mother, the daughter of Benjamin and Susan Dixon, was born in King George County, Virginia. One of Ruth's siblings died at birth. The remaining Roberts' children consisted of her six brothers and five sisters: John, Joseph, Benjamin, David, Esther, Anna, Evelyn, Daniel, Hannah, Alexander, and Violet.

Shortly after she was born, Ruth's family moved to a large home on River Road in Riverton, New Jersey, located one-quarter mile from the Delaware River. During her childhood, she and her family were active members of one of the township's prominent churches, Mt. Zion AME Church. Educated in Burlington County's public schools, Ruth attended the Cinnaminson School Number Four, a grammar school in Cinnaminson Township. Completing her secondary education in Palmyra Township, she graduated from Palmyra High School in 1936. Subsequently, she was employed as a teacher's aide and a nurse's aide.

From the time she was very small, music was an intrinsic part of Ruth's life. By the time she was school age, her parents provided her with piano lessons. Her first teacher instructed her in their home. At the age of ten, to give her more advanced training, Ruth's parents enrolled her in a music school, located on Broadway in the city of Camden. Upon mastering the fundamentals, Ruth devoted much of her time to playing religious music, particularly the hymns and spirituals that she sang in church. Later in her life, she incorporated gospel hymns into her repertoire.

When she was seventeen, Ruth became the pianist of her father's church, the Mt. Zion AME Church, located in the Kresson section of Voorhees, a rural town a few miles southeast of their home. Founded as the People's Church of Milford in 1800, written accounts of its history indicate it was first served by AME ministers from the year 1848. At that time, Ruth worked with Stanley G. Ambrose, a native of Moorestown, who was the gifted director of the church's youth choir. During the initial years of her tenure, Ruth's development was further influenced by three prominent musicians, addressed as "Professor", from Bethel AME Church in Moorestown: Daniel Ambrose (Stanley's older brother), Peter French, and Charles Robinson. Traveling the circuit of AME congregations in southern New Jersey during the Depression, they routinely instructed church musicians and choirs in order to elevate their level of performance. Eventually serving as the organist-choir director, Ruth played at Mt. Zion for more than fifty years. Under her direction for twenty-five years, their Senior Choir gave concerts at many churches throughout the area.

In 1938, Ruth married Chester English Worthington, Sr., who was also a member of the Kresson Mt. Zion AME Church. The son of Ada (Worthington) Collins, he was born in Camden on September 22, 1906. From early childhood, he was raised in West Berlin, a section of Voorhees, by his grandparents, Henry and Caroline Worthington. They, along with his mother and step-father, Levi Collins, earned a living working as sharecroppers at Coffins Corner in Delaware Township (later Cherry Hill Township). To help support his grandparents as they grew older, Chester, at age fifteen, obtained a job at Lucas Paint Works. After its purchase, the factory became part of the Sherwin Williams Company, from which he retired after fifty years of employment. When Ruth and Chester were first married, they lived in his grandparent's home. Later, they moved to Lafayette Street in Berlin, an adjacent town. They became the parents of three children: Chester Jr., Constance, and Keith.

Like Ruth, Chester, who was an accomplished vocalist, shared a great love of religious music. As a teenager, he was a soloist with the Kresson Choir, when it was directed by Stanley Ambrose, who was his distant relative. Starting in 1931, Chester received regional acclaim as a singer on the Wiley Mission program, broadcast at WCAM radio station in Camden. The show was founded by the Reverend John S. Hackett, pastor of the Wiley ME Church in the city.

After marrying and until their retirement in the 1980's, Ruth was Chester's sole accompanist. They performed on the Wiley Mission broadcast, for churches, community events, and other local radio programs. The duo were a popular attraction at the Back Home Hour, a song fest hosted by Mt. Zion that drew talented musicians and capacity audiences from the vicinity, including parishioners from St. John's Methodist Church and Greengrove Baptist Church in Berlin. Among the Worthington's other performances were frequent presentations for the Men's Federation of Burlington and Camden County, of which Chester was a member. Significantly in the 1950's, Ruth and Chester were also featured on the renowned program, the *Kershaw Hour*, working with Charles V. Kershaw and the Kershaw Royal Singers on station WKDN in Camden. Ruth's and Chester's inspirational renditions of hymns and gospel music on radio broadened their local appeal. Somewhat unique to their repertoire and of distinct interest was their performance of two hymns, published by Stanley Ambrose in 1931: *Somewhere There Is A City, I Have A Home*. Modest in appraisal of her contribution, Ruth always told people her husband was the "star" of their twosome.

In the late 1970's and early 1980's, Ruth appeared in concerts presented by the Marian Anderson Music Guild, Camden Chapter of the National Association of Negro Musicians, at the behest of her close musical associate, Henrietta Fuller Robinson, who was its current president. Although officially retired, she plays periodically at the Kresson Mt. Zion AME Church. After the loss of her husband, who died March 3, 1987, Ruth became a resident of Lindenwold, New Jersey.

YOUNG, WALTER LOUIS, SR. (1929–1992), choir director, music teacher, instrumentalist, vocalist. The second youngest of eleven children, Walter was born in Millidgeville, Georgia to Rogers and Emily (Moore) Young on June 14, 1929. While his father was also born there, his mother was a native of Atlanta, Georgia. Childhood sweethearts, Walter's parents were married in the Ebenezer Baptist Church in Millidgeville in 1915, at the ages of nineteen and fourteen, respectively. His ten siblings were born between 1916 and 1933: James, Chester, Josephine, Alice, Nathaniel, John, Joseph, Olivia,

146

Odessa, and Ola Mae. To support the family, which included Walter's paternal grandmother, his father worked as a share-cropper. A fine seamstress who sewed most of their clothing, his mother stayed at home to care for their large family.

In 1934, the midst of the Depression years, Walter's family moved to Camden, New Jersey. When they first arrived, they stayed with his mother's brother, Willie Mills, in a nineteen room house at 424 South Fourth Street. Although finding work was difficult, Walter's father eventually obtained jobs with the Campbell Soup Company, and the federal government's Works Progress Administration road's construction project . He was later employed by the Pennsylvania Railroad, working for the company until his retirement.

Stricken with diphtheria as a small child, Walter was legally blind and walked with an unsteady gait. Between ages six and eight, he was treated for his infirmity at the Lakeland Sanitarium, a hospital that provided medical care for individuals with communicable diseases, in Atco, New Jersey. During his lengthy recovery, Walter lived at the facility on weekdays and visited his family on weekends. To improve his vision, his doctors prescribed for him eyeglasses with strong corrective lenses. Because they were impressed by his quick mind and charming personality, the medical staff also gave him books that he used to teach himself the fundamentals of reading and arithmetic. As a result of his precocity, when his parents enrolled him in the Mt. Vernon Public School in Camden, Walter entered the third grade at the appropriate age of eight. Subsequently transferred, he completed grammar school at the John Greenleaf Whittier School.

From early childhood, Walter also displayed an inherent musical ability that equaled his intellectual gifts. With access to a piano at home and at the sanitarium, he started teaching himself to play at age six. In school, music was his favorite class. On Sundays, he and his siblings loved singing in the choir at Mickle Baptist Church (renamed New Mickle Baptist Church) in Camden. Since his parents could not afford to give him lessons, Walter, by the age of ten, started studying music theory by reading books in the Music Division of the library of the South Jersey Law School and College of South Jersey, located at 224 Federal Street in the City. Several of the librarians and professors, likewise impressed by his intelligence, ensured his regular entry to the building.

Shortly after becoming a student at Clara Burroughs Junior High School, Walter sustained a serious injury that disrupted his schooling. While he and a friend were moving a neighbor's piano, it fell from their grip and crushed his legs. Remarkably, although unable to attend classes for eighteen months, he caught up with his studies. After graduating from junior high school, Walter entered the Woodrow Wilson High School. While he was in high school, his brothers, Chester, Nathaniel, and Joseph, recruited him to form a quartet, calling themselves the Gospel Messengers. As a member of the ensemble, he gained valuable experience performing gospel music in a variety of public venues. However, within three years, Walter's preference for singing traditional hymns, spirituals, and classical music caused him to leave the group to pursue his own interests.

In 1946 after turning seventeen, Walter decided to drop out of high school to start working. Later that year, he enlisted in the U.S. Army. During two years of service, he completed his secondary education, attended communications school at Fort Knox, Tennessee, and worked as a decoder. Upon his discharge Walter returned to Camden. Having also attended a watchmaking school, he and an associate, William Martin, opened a jewelry and watch and clock repair store at Seventh Street and Kaighn Avenue. In operation during most of 1949, they closed the business after they were robbed.

In November of 1951, Walter married Mildred Morgan, who was a native of Moorestown, New Jersey, at the Second Baptist Church in Moorestown. They had met at a church social at the Bethany Baptist Church in nearby Burlington City. Residing in Camden, the couple became parents of seven children, all musically endowed: Denise, Lorna, Claudia, Walter Jr., Clark, Ronald, and Kevin. Walter supported his family by working in construction during the day and for the railroad at night. After their youngest child was enrolled in the second grade, Mildred was employed by the Camden School Board, as a teacher's aide and subsequently, a clerical worker.

Because of his great passion for music, Walter made it the daily focus of his family's life, first by providing himself and his children

148

with lessons, then performing with them in ensembles. In the late 1950's, he and his daughters studied stringed instruments, the violin, viola, violoncello, and bass, with Robert Williams, a local music teacher. They practiced together as a quartet. To foster their considerable talent, Walter sent his children for additional training at the Settlement Music School in Philadelphia, Pennsylvania. Through his encouragement, each of them studied at least two instruments, becoming proficient playing the piano, organ, and woodwind instruments. This led to daily performances as an "orchestra" under Walter's direction. One year, he also assisted the music teacher at his children's elementary school, the Northeast-Sewell School in Camden, by training the marching band.

In 1962, Walter started his most celebrated work as a conductor, and expanded his work into the community. That year, his daughters Denise and Lorna, and their friends, Karen and Elizabeth Robinson, asked him to train them to sing so they could audition for a new glee club at school. Under Walter's tutelage, the lessons quickly evolved into the creation of a thirty-two voice choral ensemble, initially called the Young People's Choral Ensemble. Renamed Young's Choral Ensemble, in his honor, the group consisted of his four eldest children, several of their classmates, and other children in the neighborhood.

From the first rehearsal, Walter trained the vocalists, who ranged in age from eight to late teens, to sing sacred and secular choral works in four and eight part harmony. In twice weekly rehearsals, he instructed them in basic theory as well. The group's repertoire consisted of several challenging classical compositions, including Handel's *Messiah,* as well as selections in German and Latin. With his daughters as accompanists, Walter and the ensemble started giving concerts in churches in Camden and in the vicinity. An immediate success, they were invited for repeat performances at several places: Kaighn Avenue Baptist Church, in the city; the Haddonfield UM Church, in Haddonfield; the Hospitality Nursing Home, in Cherry Hill. They also sang with the Camden City Orchestra, whose conductor, at the time, was Alex English.

Gradually, Walter and the choral ensemble were invited to perform in more prestigious venues. One such notable appearance was an audition on the television program, the *Ted Mack Original Amateur Hour*, on December 22, 1968. The following year, with the sponsorship of the Metropolitan Opera Singers of New York, Young's Choral Ensemble sang in Brush Brook Park in Newark, New Jersey on August 24, 1969, before an audience that included the State's Governor, Richard Hughes. In the late 1960's and early 1970's the group traveled extensively, throughout New Jersey and Pennsylvania, and to Bridgeport, Connecticut.

Gaining the financial support of patrons allowed Walter to award scholarships for music lessons at the Settlement Music School to several members of Young's Choral Ensemble. This opportunity for further study, combined with their rich experiences in the ensemble, helped motivate a significant number, including his eldest daughters, to pursue professional music careers. Denise Young taught piano and theory in her own music studio and served as the choir director of Faith Baptist Church in Camden. After joining the faculty of the University of the Virgin Islands, then earning a doctorate in music, Lorna Young, notably, performed in concert in the Soviet Union. Annabelle English became a music teacher in the public schools of southern New Jersey. Another outstanding member, Carla Benson, sang as a back up singer for Patti LaBelle, and worked as a studio musician for Philadelphia International Records, the well-known Philadelphia, Pennsylvania recording company founded by Leon Huff and Kenny Gamble. Young's Choral Ensemble disbanded in the mid 1970's, when several of the singers reached adulthood.

Propelled into the musical spotlight, Walter's fine reputation brought him invitations to conduct other choirs in the presentation of sacred music at churches in southern New Jersey and Philadelphia within this same period. In Camden, he served as a guest conductor for special programs at the following churches: Parkside UM Church, Kaighn Avenue Baptist Church, Broadway UM Church. In 1978, Walter became a co-founder and principal director of the Ecumenical Choir of Camden, New Jersey & Vicinity, an assemblage of the area's leading musicians comprised to honor James Wheeler. For that project, he worked in close association with Lois Custis Harris, Jesse I. Hamilton, Jr., Mary Morrow, and Vaughn Archie. He continued

150

conducting until shortly before his death. Walter, an active member of the Hampton University Choir Directors and Organists Guild, attended the joint annual June meeting of the Hampton University Ministers' Conference and Annual Choir Directors and Organists Guild Workshop.

Primarily a self-taught musician, Walter was greatly respected for his distinguished accomplishments. In appreciation for his work, his peers honored him in a special concert at Kaighn Avenue Baptist Church on March 17, 1991. After a serious illness, Walter died on May 6, 1992 at the age of sixty-two.

The Senior Choir of Kaighn Avenue Baptist Church in Camden has a marvelous musical legacy, dating to the early twentieth century. In the 1930's, the heyday of James Marshall Wheeler, organist, and Phillip Johnson, director, the ensemble won three consecutive statewide competitions at the Bordentown School, and a trophy cup. Chris Payne, who served forty-four years, and his successor, Michael Jackson, dedicated themselves to preserving time-honored traditions in presenting sacred music. Generations of Kaighn Avenue Bapist's choristers have done the same. Back, left to right: Lawrence Gibson, C. Nathaniel Thompson, Joseph "Sonny" Wilson, Lois Smith. Center, left to right: Wilbert Jenkins, Anthony Taylor, Mary Burell, Frances Williams, Constance Hampton, Gladys Godfrey, Sarah Hamlett, Carolyn Wharton, Verniece Godfrey, Mary Braswell, Edna Smith. Front, left to right: Michael Jackson, organist-choir director, Angela Shields. Photograph, by Ron Jackson. From the collection of Carolyn Cordelia Williams.

PART THREE

Appendixes, Bibliography, Index

APPENDIX A

Labor patterns for African American female musicians & music
teachers 1910–1950

U.S. Population Census			
	Total professionals	Musicians- Music teachers	% total
1910	30071	2347	7.80%
1920	39127	2150	5.49%
1930	63027 [1]	2836	4.50%
1940	69469 [2]	2381 [2]	3.43% [2]
1950	104280 [2]	3210 [2]	3.01% [2]

New Jersey Population Census			
	Total professionals	Musicians- Music teachers	% total
1910	266	77	28.95%
1920	388	80	20.62%
1930	852	107	12.56%
1940	798 [2]	75 [2]	9.40% [2]
1950	1635	75	4.59%

[1] = professional non-recreation and recreation and amusement
categories
[2] employed and seeking work
Compiled from Department of Commerce Census data

APPENDIX B

Labor patterns for White female musicians & music teachers
1910–1950

U.S. Population Census			
	Total professionals	Musicians-Music teachers	% total
1910	748758 [1]	82096 [1]	10.96% [1]
1920	976821 [1]	70492 [1]	7.22% [1]
1930	1684599 [2]	76553 [2]	4.54% [2]
1940	1448571 [4]	61261 [4]	4.22% [4]
1950	1864590 [4]	79680 [4]	4.27% [4]

New Jersey Population Census			
	Total professionals	Musicians-Music teachers	% total
1910	18700 [1]	2293 [1]	12.26% [1]
1920	27817 [1]	1969 [1]	7.08% [1]
1930	50957 [2]	2342 [2]	4.60% [2]
1940	52273 [4]	1689 [4]	3.23% [4]
1950	62483 [4]	1874 [4]	3.00% [4]

[1] parentage=native born, foreign born, and mixed
[2] native born and foreign born
[3] = professional non-recreation and recreation and amusement categories
[4] = employed and seeking work
Compiled from Department of Commerce Census data

<u>APPENDIX C</u>

Labor patterns for African American male musicians & music
teachers 1910–1950

U.S. Population Census			
	Total professionals	Musicians- Music teachers	% total
1910	39400	3259	8.27%
1920	41056	3752	9.14%
1930	72898[1]	7747	10.63%
1940	57674[2]	6776[2]	11.75%[2]
1950	75090[2]	6330[2]	8.43%[2]

New Jersey Population Census			
	Total professionals	Musicians- Music teachers	% total
1910	564	100	17.73%
1920	738	121	16.40%
1930	1891	239	12.64%
1940	1164[2]	208[2]	17.87%[2]
1950	1701	158	9.29%

[1] = professional non-recreation and recreation and amusement
categories
[2] employed and seeking work
Compiled from Department of Commerce Census data

APPENDIX D

Labor patterns for White male musicians & music teachers
1910–1950

U.S. Population Census			
	Total professionals	Musicians-Music teachers	% total
1910	891,656 [1]	51,509 [1]	5.78% [1]
1920	1,083,988 [1]	53750 [1]	5.11% [1]
1930	1534749 [2,3]	76401 [2]	4.98% [2]
1940	1,896,919 [4]	77923 [4]	4.11% [4]
1950	2,881,230 [4]	73110 [4]	2.54% [4]

New Jersey Population Census			
	Total professionals	Musicians-Music teachers	% total
1910	24355 [1]	2033 [1]	8.35% [1]
1920	41147 [1]	2068 [1]	5.03% [1]
1930	73199 [2]	3320 [2]	4.54% [2]
1940	85518	2977	3.48%
1950	132610	2539	1.9%

[1] parentage=native born, foreign born, and mixed
[2] native born and foreign born
[3] = professional non-recreation and recreation and amusement categories
[4] = employed and seeking work
Compiled from Department of Commerce Census data

157

APPENDIX E

Woodbury Choral Society, established October 1936
S. Edward Davis, founder-director

Tony Allen	Jean Eldridge
Alvinia Bagby	Dorothy Davis Estrada
Sarah Bagby	Robin H. Farguhar
Harold Bailey	Gloria Fisher [3]
Charlotte Barringer	Harold Fisher
Jadie Barringer	Walter Frisby
Pauline Baylor	John Gaines
Viola Bell	Amos Galloway [3]
Brenda Benson	Phyllis Gibson
Sylvia Blake	William A. Glaser
Harriet Bowman	Marguerite Gould
Clara E. Brazier [2]	Helen Graves
Charles W. Brown [1]	Frank Greene
E. Lucille Brown [3]	Joyce Greene
Frances Brown	Robert Greene
Douglas Browne [3]	Eleanor Hailey
Sylvanus Browne, Jr. [3]	Jeanette Hall
Victor Browne	Richard Hailey
Lillian Bruner	Constance Hardy
William Bullock	Doris Harmon
Esther Burrell [3]	Rose Harris [3]
Peter N. Butler	Argenia Hawkins
S. Leroy Chandler	Charles E. Hill, Jr. [1,3]
Mabel A. Clifton	Elvinia Hill
Blanche Corsey	Sylvia Hill
Roland Corsey	Jesse I. Hamilton, Jr.
Herman F. Curtis [3]	Mabel Harris
Rodney Davis	Ludie Mae Hill
Theresa S. Davis [3]	Milton Hinton
Pearl S. Dorsey	Delores Holmes
Sagamore H. Dorsey [3]	Rutha Holmes [3]

Compiled from program books dated: 28 May 1937; 19 May 1939; 1 Jun 1940; 14 Jun 1942; 24 May 1947; 21 May 1949; 26 May 1951; 17 May 1958; 3 March 1962 (25th Anniversary celebration). No concerts were given during WW II era, i.e. 1943–1946. No data for 1938, 1948, 1952–1957, 1959–1961, and 1963–1970's. Whenever possible, female members' maiden and married surnames were combined to avoid duplication.
[1] assistant conductor, [2] accompanist, [3] officer

APPENDIX E (cont.)

Genevieve Ingram	Robert Schools
Vivian Ingram	Evelyn V. Sellers [3]
Argenetta Jackson	Irene H. Smith [3]
James Jackson	Frances Starks
Helen V. Jenkins	Audrey Stevenson
Hazel Johnson	Catherine Stevenson
Horace Johnson	Constance Stevenson [3]
Margery Brown Johnson	David Stevenson
Nellie L. Kehlet [1]	Pearl Stevenson
Joyce B. Kennedy	Margaret Stewart
Hilda King	William Suitor
Eugene Kirby	Mildred Sye
Pauline Lawrence [3]	Brenda Taylor
Genevieve R. Lee	Richard Taylor
Jun Lockett	Wayne Triplett
Mary Lockett	Earle Truxson
Earl Lockwood	Helen Tunstall
Carl Mann	Ann Vesenka
Daniel Martin	Evelyn Vincent
Dorothy Martin	George Garner Waples [1]
Jean C. Martin [3]	Audrey Warren
Lewis Martin	John Warren
Mary Moody [3]	John Alfred Washington
Veronica Moody	John Amos Washington Sr. [3]
James M. Moss	Lillian Washington
Christopher Payne	Harry Williams
Corrine Pope [2]	Sarah C. Williams [2]
Genevieve Ricco	William L. Williams [3]
Viola Robbins [3]	Estella Woodland
Virginia Robinson	Madeline Wright
Mary O. Sample	

Complied from program books dated: 28 May 1937; 19 May 1939; 1 Jun 1940; 14 Jun 1942; 24 May 1947; 21 May 1949; 26 May 1951; 17 May 1958; 3 March 1962 (25th Anniversary celebration). No concerts were given during WW II era, i.e. 1943–1946. No data for 1938, 1948, 1952–1957, 1959–1961, and 1963–1970's. Whenever possible, female members' maiden and married surnames were combined to avoid duplication.

[1] assistant conductor, [2] accompanist, [3] officer

APPENDIX F

Campbell Soup Male Glee Club, founded November 17, 1942
Sue Smith McDonald, director Hyland B. Frisby, manager

James Alston [f]
Evanda Bagby [f]
Alexander Barber [f]
Samuel Benson [f]
Charles Brown
Clifton Brown [f]
John Brown
W. Brown
Michael Bryan [f]
Elwood Bryant [f]
W. W. Burnside [f]
Harrison Burton [f]
John Byrd [f]
Charles Campbell
Frank Coleman [f]
John B. Coney
Raymond Cox [f]
Charles Dorsey [f]
Charles Everett [f]
Thomas Freeman
Hyland Frisby [f]
Sidney Goodman [f]
John E. Gray [f]
Roland Hall [f]
Robert Hamilton [f]
Daniel Harrington [f]
Sylvester Harris [f]
W. E. Henderson [f]
James Hinton

Eugene Ingram [f]
James Ingram [f]
John Jackson [f]
Edward Jenkins [f]
Leon Jenkins [f]
James Jones [f]
Fernando McLeod [f]
Lloyd Mitchell
George Mitchum [f]
John Moody [f]
Charles Mosley [f]
Anthony Portlock [f]
Carroll Primas [f]
George Riley
Robert Schaeffer
Alexander Sessoma [f]
James Shaw [f]
Alonzo Smith [f]
Harry Small [f]
Elwood Stafford
Robert Stafford [f]
Louis Stukes
Clement Truitt [f]
Robert Tunnell [f]
John Walls [f]
Howard Ways [f]
Charles Williams [f]
Elijah Williams [f]
Bruce White [f]

[f] = founding members. Compiled from the Campbell Soup Company's in-house publications, *Soup Tureen* and *Campbell People*. See bibliography for dates. Since certain issues were not available, compilation may be incomplete.

APPENDIX G

Young's Choral Ensemble, established 1962

Walter Louis Young Sr., director
Lorna Young, Denise Young, accompanists

Carla Benson
Lorenzo Broadwater
William Chew
Douglas Crawley
Annabelle English
Rose English
Ed Furgerson
Doris Grady
William Grimmer
Lela Ingalls
Jonathan Johnson
Bonnie Lipscomb
Dorothy Lipscomb

Charlotte Martin
Debbie Moore
John Peoples
Elizabeth Marcia Robinson
Karen E. Robinson
Curnell Thompson
Vernon Wallace
Roberta West
Marc Williamson
Kathleen Wilson
Claudia Young
Walter Louis Young, Jr.

Source: Mildred Morgan Young

APPENDIX H

Marian Anderson Music Guild, Camden Chapter
of the National Association of Negro Musicians,
established 1971

co-founders: Isabelle Crews Collins, Reverend J. Ferman Little

Debra Bates	Tina Jones [5]
Louis Beeks, Jr.	J. Ferman Little [1]
Rosetta Boyd	Mary E. Little
Theodore H. Brooks	Ida Lofton
Barbara Brown	Jacqueline Mitchell
Catherine Bullock [5]	Blanche M. Moore
Karen Bullock	Bertha Nelms
Janet Bussey [5]	Arzulia O'Neal [4]
Alberta Darius Clark	Esau O'Neal [3]
Lisa Clark [5]	Serena Orange [5]
Carrie Langford Collier	Laura Beeks Outlaw
Ida Conaway	Melvin Pugh
Dorothy Conley	Blanchard W. Robinson
Alice Cook	Henrietta Fuller Robinson [2]
Esther Cook [5]	Mary O. Robinson
Eva Cook [5]	Kay Scott
Eula M. Cordy	Gladys Still
Reverend Mattie Dotson	Catherine Streater
Theresa Epps	Eva T. Stroud
Delores Friend	Delores Taylor
Josephine Gantt	Wallace Vann [5]
Mary Griffin	Essie Holmes Voorhees
Tabitha Griffin [5]	Martina Watson
Lois K. Harris	Carol Wims
Lottie Price James	Claudia Green Young
Alberta C. Johnson	Maxine Evers

[1] president 1971–1977, [2] president 1977–1987, [3] president 1987–1994, [4] president 1994–1996, [5] youth and junior members. Note: Rachel Merrill was elected president May 1996. Data incomplete for years 1971-1977 and 1987-1996. Source: membership records, program books.

APPENDIX I

Ecumenical Choir of Camden & Vicinity, established 1978

co-directors: Lois K. Harris[1], Jesse I. Hamilton, Jr., Mary Morrow, Vaughn Archie, Walter L. Young Sr., Wanda Buell, Robert S. Mayes

instrumentalists: Lois K. Harris, George Buell, Juanita Fernandez, Allen Foster, Lorna Young, Crystal Allison, Robin Tolbert

Alice Adams	Rose English[2]
Crete Allison[2,3]	Mabel Farmer[2]
Crystal Allison	Joseph Fennell
Maybell Amado	James Ferguson
Vaughn Archie	Juanita Fernandez
Virginia Bagwell	Vernon Ford
Paulette Banks	Andrew Foster
Mercedes Beecham	Doris L. Freeman
Alease Bell	John C. Gaines
James Benson	Mary Gaines
Lillie Beverly	Josephine Gantt
Joyce Boston[3]	Josephine Gibbs
Rebecca Brent[3]	Audrey Givens
Evelyn Brownlee	Holton Hackett[2]
Theodore Brooks	Mabel Hall
James Burch	Helen Hamilton[3]
Melvin Burt[2]	Jesse I. Hamilton, Jr.
Edra Chandler[2]	Paul Hamilton[2]
Vanessa Christmas[2]	Vanessa Hamilton
Mary Coleman	Georgia Hampton[2,3]
Edith Curley	Rose Henley
Candace Davis	Alexander J. Hines[2]
Lawrence Davis	James Hinson[2]
Acey Elsey[2]	Bernice Holmes

[1] founder, [2] soloists, [3] officers

Compiled from 1978-1982 program books.

APPENDIX I (cont.)

Rubin Horcey

Charles Huff

Margaret Hunt

Lillian Ingram [3]

N. Henry Ingram Sr. [3]

Beatrice Jackson [2, 3]

Rochelle Jackson

Beatrice Johnson

Doris Johnson

Morris Johnson

Bonnie L. Jones

Leatrice Jones

Alfred Kincey

Catherine Lewis [3]

Dorothy Lipscomb

William Martin

Robert S. Mayes

Elizabeth Morgan

Mary Morrow

Lena Murrell

John Nichols Sr.

Robert Norwood [2]

Alethia Prater [2]

Bernice Randall

Viola Rawlins [3]

Carolyn T. Richardson

Elizabeth Marcia Robinson [3]

Frances Satchell [2]

Charles Scott

Corrine Scott [3]

Thelma Scott

Caroline Smith

Jeanine Smith

Gloria Spratley

Juanita Starks

Eugene Tatem

Anthony Taylor

Caroline E. Torrence

Lorraine Upshaw [3]

Vernon Wallace [2]

Jacqueline C. Warren

Claudius Wheeler

Elandues Wheeler

Cornelia Wiggins [2]

Eunice Williams [3]

Raymond Wilmer

Joseph Wilson

Christine Wing

Rosezell Woods

Lorna Young

Walter L. Young

[1] founder, [2] soloists, [3] officers

Compiled from 1978-1982 program books.

BIBLIOGRAPHY

Primary Sources

A. Interviews and Personal Communications

Allison, Theodora. Interview questionnaire to and telephone conversations with C.C. Williams. 10 Aug , 18 Aug, and 5 Sep 1995.

Blair, Ellen. Interview with C.C. Williams via telephone. 9 Aug 1995. Transcription, personal collection of C.C. Williams.

Blake, Marie. Telephone conversation with H.F. Robinson. 1992.

Buck, Marion. Telephone conversation with C.C. Williams. 10 Aug 1995.

Buell, George. Interview with C.C. Williams. Moorestown, NJ, 3 Aug 1995.

Collins, Isabelle Crews. Interview with C.C. Williams. Camden, NJ, 20 Jul 1995 and 24 Jul 1995. Audiotape, personal collection of C.C. Williams.

Curley, Edith. Interview with C.C. Williams. Camden, NJ, 27 Jul 1995. Audiotape, personal collection of C.C. Williams.

Davis, Elmira Howard. Interview with C.C. Williams. West Deptford, NJ, 24 Aug 1995. Audiotape, personal collection of C.C. Williams.

Durham, Alice Baughn. Interview questionnaire to H.F. Robinson. 1983. Interview with C.C. Williams. Berlin, NJ, 24 Jul 1995. Audiotape, personal collection of C.C. Williams.

Estrada, Dorothy Davis. Interview with C.C. Williams. West Deptford, NJ, 24 Aug 1995. Audiotape, personal collection of C.C. Williams.

Evers, Maxine Monroe. Interview questionnaire to H.F. Robinson. 1983. Interview questionnaire to C.C. Williams. 18 Sep 1995. Telephone conversation with C.C. Williams. 10 Nov 1995.

Fernandez (Fernanders), Juanita. Interview with C.C. Williams via telephone. 9 Aug 1995. Transcription, personal collection of C.C. Williams.

Foster, Allen Sr. Interview with C.C. Williams. Philadelphia, PA, 4 Dec 1995. Transcription, personal collection of C.C. Williams.

Fraction, Edward A. Jr. Interview with C.C. Williams. Camden, NJ, 11 Jul 1995. Audiotape, personal collection of C.C. Williams.

Gantt, Ruth Brown. Interview with C.C. Williams. West Atco, NJ, 16 Aug 1995. Audiotape, personal collection of C.C. Williams.

Gibson, Evelyn C. Telephone conversation with C.C. Williams. 10 Aug 1995.

Gilmore, Virginia Hackett. Telephone conversation with C.C. Williams. 15 Dec 1995.

Givens, Audrey Canois. Interview with C.C. Williams via telephone. 9 Aug and 30 Aug 1995. Transcription, personal collection of C.C. Williams.

Golden, Odessa Young. Interview with C.C. Williams. Cherry Hill, NJ, 18 Aug 1995. Audiotape, personal collection of C.C. Williams.

Hamilton, Jesse I. Jr. Interview questionnaire to H.F. Robinson. 1983. Interview with C.C. Williams. Magnolia, NJ, 25 Jul 1995. Audiotape, personal collection of C.C. Williams.

Harris, Lois K. Interview with C.C. Williams. Camden, NJ, 21 Aug 1995. Audiotape, personal collection of C.C. Williams.

Hightower, Dorothy Ashbridge. Telephone conversation with C.C. Williams. 2 Apr 1996.

Holland, Jacqueline. Interview with C.C. Williams. Philadelphia, PA. 9 Sep 1995. Transcription, personal collection of C.C. Williams.

Hudson, Albert and Ramona. Interviews with H.F. Robinson. 1983–1992. Interview with C.C. Williams. Pennsauken, NJ, 21 Jul 1995 Audiotape, personal collection of C.C. Williams.

Ingram, N. Henry Jr. Interview with C.C. Williams. Voorhees, NJ, 22 Sep 1995. Audiotape, personal collection of C.C. Williams.

Ingram, N. Henry, Sr. Interview questionnaire to H.F. Robinson. 1983.

Jester, Eva. Tel. convers. with C.C. Williams. 27 Aug 1995, 27 Jan 1997.

Jeter-Bey, Eugene. Telephone conversation with C.C. Williams. 17 Sep 1995.

Johnson, Edith. Telephone conversation with C.C. Williams. 22 Aug 1995.

Johnson, Evangeline. Interview with C.C. Williams. Camden, NJ, 28 Jul 1995. Transcription, personal collection of C.C. Williams.

Jones, Maryetta Hopkins. Interview with H.F. Robinson. 1985.

Little, J. Ferman. Interview with C.C. Williams. Camden, NJ, 28 Jul 1995. Audiotape, personal collection of C.C. Williams.

Lewis, Granville Jr. Telephone conversation with C.C. Williams. 5 Dec 1995.

McDonald, Sue Smith. Interview questionnaire to H.F. Robinson. 1983.

O'Neal, Esau. Interview questionnaire to H.F. Robinson. 1983. Interview with C.C. Williams. Lawnside, NJ, 31 Jul 1995. Audiotape, personal collection of C.C. Williams.

Outlaw, Laura Beeks. Interview questionnaire to H.F. Robinson. 1985.

Payne, Henry. Interview with C.C. Williams. Swedesboro, NJ, 11 Aug 1995. Audiotape, personal collection of C.C. Williams.

Payne, James. Interview with C.C. Williams. Swedesboro, NJ, 11 Aug 1995. Audiotape, personal collection of C.C. Williams.

Puggsley, Carline Lewis. Interview questionnaire to H.F. Robinson. 1983.

Richardson, Iona Davis. Interview questionnaire to H.F. Robinson. 1983. Interview with C.C. Williams via telephone. 3 Aug 1995. Transcription, personal collection of C.C. Williams.

Robinson, Henrietta Fuller. Interview with C.C. Williams. Camden, NJ, May and Jun, 1994. Audiotape, personal collection of C.C. Williams.

Shaw, Ada. Interview with C.C. Williams. Camden, NJ, 2 Aug 1995. Au diotape, personal collection of C.C. Williams.

Smith, Niramay. Telephone conversation with C.C. Williams. 26 Jun 1996.

Still, Emily Jones. Telephone conversation with C.C. Williams. 31 Aug 1995.

Sykes, Hazel. Telephone conversation with C.C. Williams. 18 Aug 1995.

Taylor, Sadye Gibson. Telephone conversation with C.C. Williams. 8 Aug 1995.

Voorhees, Essie Holmes. Interview questionnaire to H.F. Robinson. 1983. Interview with C.C. Williams. Camden, NJ, 6 Jul 1995, 13 Jul 1995, 26 Jul 1995. Audiotape, personal collection of C.C. Williams.

Waples, Gretchen Branche. Interview with C.C. Williams. Camden, NJ, 7 Aug 1995. Audiotape, personal collection of C.C. Williams.

Williams, Claudia Young. Interview with C.C. Williams. Cherry Hill, NJ, 18 Aug 1995. Audiotape, personal collection of C.C. Williams.

Willis, Ola Mae Young. Interview with C.C. Williams. Cherry Hill, NJ, 18 Aug 1995. Audiotape, personal collection of C.C. Williams.

Wilson, Rosanna "Rose" Payne. Interview with H.F. Robinson. Camden, NJ. 1985.

Winchester, Mary. Telephone conversation with C.C. Williams. 3 Aug 1995.

Woods, Della. Telephone conversation with C.C. Williams. 17 Aug 1995.

Wormack, Mabel Hopkins. Interview questionnaire to H.F. Robinson. 1985.

Worthington, Chester Jr. Interview with C.C. Williams. Chesilhurst, NJ, 29 Aug 1995. Audiotape, personal collection of C.C. Williams.

Worthington, Ruth Roberts. Interview questionnaire to H.F. Robinson. 1985.

Young, Claudia Green. Telephone conversation with C.C. Williams. 18 Aug 1995.

Young, Mildred Morgan. Interview with C.C. Williams. Cherry Hill, NJ, 18 Aug 1995. Audiotape, personal collection of C.C. Williams.

B. Manuscript Collections

Afro-American Historical and Cultural Museum, Philadelphia, PA. Doris and W. Leon Bullock Collection. Program books from the Dra Mu Opera

Company, 1945–48, Pro Arts Society, Encore Opera Company, and various churches.

> George Everett Walton Collection. Program books and notices for several musical ensembles in Philadelphia and southern New Jersey, 1908–1960, including Hunton Symphony Orchestra, Dra Mu Opera Company, Philadelphia Concert Orchestra.

Camden County Historical Society, Camden, NJ.

> Gamma Nu Zeta Chapter, Zeta Phi Beta Sorority, Inc. 1976. *Life and History of Black Americans in Camden County New Jersey*. Scrapbook.
> Camden City Directories. (See Newspapers and Periodicals below).

Campbell Soup Company Archives, Camden, NJ.

> Collection of in-house publications. *Soup Tureen*, December 1942. *Soup Tureen*, Jun 1943. *Soup Tureen*, December 1943. *Soup Tureen*, November 1945. *Campbell People*, November 1947. *Campbell People*, September 1949. *Campbell People*, November 1952. *Campbell People*, December 1952. *Campbell People*, May 1953. *Campbell People*, April 1959.

New Jersey State Archives, Trenton, NJ.

> Department of Education. New Jersey Manual Training and Industrial School for Colored Youth Collection (the Bordentown Training School).

Private Collections and Personal Papers.

> Brown, Emily Lucken. Music, programs from student recitals, personal appearances. Several photographs of the *Kershaw Royal Singers* and the *Borden Bellringers*. Courtesy of Ruth Brown Gantt.
>
> Collins, Isabelle M. Crews. Concert appearances, promotional materials, teaching records, music. Records and correspondence pertaining to membership and offices held in the National Association of Negro Musicians.
>
> Davis, S. Edward and Elmira. Woodbury Choral Society program books, correspondence, business papers. Awards, citations, and photographs, including one of Woodbury Choral Society and the Youth Choir of the Bethel AME Church, Woodbury, NJ.
>
> Dittimus, Theda. Memorabilia and obituary of Mabel Hopkins Wormack.
>
> Durham, Alice Baughn. Music, program booklets, newspaper clippings, teaching records. Includes program book, *Judimar School of Dance Annual Performance*, May 31–Jun 1, 1951.
>
> Hamilton, Jesse I. Jr. Correspondence, newspaper clippings, music,

program booklets. Includes personal papers of Jesse I. Hamilton Sr. and program books of the Ecumenical Choir of Camden & Vicinity.

Harris, Lois K. Custis. Music, program booklets, newspaper clippings. Ecumenical Choir of Camden & Vicinity Concert Album.

Hightower, Dorothy Ashbridge. Obituaries of Myrtle Van Buren Watson and William Watson.

Holmes, Roberta Jones. Teaching records, music, promotional materials. Business papers for music retail operations and studios in Camden and Newark, NJ. Courtesy of Essie Holmes Voorhees.

Hudson, Albert. Published music of Stanley G. Ambrose.

Little, J. Ferman. Music, concert and recital notices, program books. Records regarding establishment of the National Association of Negro Musicians, Camden Chapter (Marian Anderson Music Guild). Photographs of the Elder Solomon Michaux and the Church of God Cross Choir. Phonorecords.

McDonald, Sue Smith. Correspondence, newspaper clippings, programs and promotional materials from concerts, student recitals, and opera productions in southern New Jersey, Philadelphia, and other locales. Photographs of the Campbell Soup Company Male Glee Club, the McDonald Mixed Chorus, soloists of the Wharton-McDonald Opera Workshop. Courtesy of Eva P. Jester.

Riley, Floyd M. Valuable collection of obituaries, principally residents in the vicinity of Berlin, NJ.

Robinson, Henrietta Fuller. Extensive collection of music, teaching records, recital and concert notices, personal and business correspondence, and program booklets. Features items from local musicians, southern New Jersey churches, professional associations and civic organizations: Camden YWCA; Marian Anderson Music Guild, Camden branch National Association of Negro Musicians, Inc.; Association for the Study of Afro-American Life and History, South Jersey Branch. Photographs, slides, and scrapbooks, 1950's–1990's.

Shaw, Gilbert. History of the Ferry Avenue United Methodist Church.

Voorhees, Essie Holmes. Music, concert notices, programs, promotional materials, student recitals, scrapbook collection of memorabilia and photographs.

Wilson, Rose Payne. Personal papers, family bible, photographs, death certificate. Courtesy of Niramay Smith.

Worthington, Ruth and Chester A., Sr. Music, church program booklets, photographs.

Young, Walter Louis, Sr. Scrapbook consisting of biographical material, concert appearances, newspaper clippings, awards and citations. Courtesy of Mildred Morgan Young.

C. Newspapers and Periodicals

The Courier Post, 1949–1990. Print and microfilm.
Howe, C.E. Co. 1882–1912. *Camden City and County Directory.* Philadelphia, PA: C.E. Howe Co. Print.
———. 1913–1922. *Boyd's Greater Camden City Directory.* Philadelphia, PA: C.E. Howe Co. Print.
"Meet Resident...Sue McDonald." *Word from Home.* Philadelphia: Simpson House. Winter, 1990–1991, pp. 3–4. Newsletter.
The Philadelphia Afro-American, 1970–1985. Print and microfilm.
The Philadelphia Independent, 1930–1960. Print and microfilm.
The Philadelphia Tribune, 1912–1970. Microfilm.
Polk Co. 1923–1950. *Polk's Greater Camden City Directory.* Philadelphia, PA: Polk Co. Print.
Research Publications. 1984. *City Directories of the United States: Segment IV, 1902-1935, Philadelphia, Pennsylvania.* Woodbridge, CT. Microfilm.

D. Government Publications

Department of the Interior, Bureau of Education. 1917. *Negro Education: A Study of the Private and Higher Schools for Colored People in the United States.* Washington, D.C.: Government Printing Office. Bulletin 1916, number 39, volume II.
New Jersey Department of State. 1915. *Census of the State of New Jersey.* Microfilm.
U.S. Department of Commerce, Bureau of the Census. 1870–1920. *U.S. Census Population Schedules.* Microfilm.
———. 1914. *Thirteenth Census of the United States Taken in the Year 1910: Volume IV, Population 1910, Occupation Statistics.* Washington: Government Printing Office.
———. 1918. *Negro Population 1790–1915.* Washington: Government Printing Office.
———. 1923. *Fourteenth Census of the United States: Taken in the Year 1920, Volume IV, Population, 1920, Occupations.* Washington, D.C.: Government Printing Office.

———. 1933. *Fifteenth Census of the United States: 1930, Population Volume IV, Occupation by States, Giving Statistics for Cities of 25,000 or more.* Washington, D.C.: Government Printing Office.

———. 1933. *Fifteenth Census of the United States: 1930, Population Volume V, General Report on Occupations.* Washington, D.C.: Government Printing Office.

———. 1935. *Negroes in the United States 1920–32.* Washington, D.C.: Government Printing Office.

———. 1943. *Sixteenth Census of the United States: 1940, Population Volume III, The Labor Force, Occupation, Industry, Employment, and Income, Part I: The United States Summary.* Washington: United States Government Printing Office.

———. 1943. *Sixteenth Census of the United States: 1940, Population Volume III, The Labor Force, Occupation, Industry, Employment, and Income, Part IV: Nebraska-Oregon.* Washington: United States Government Printing Office.

———. 1952. *A Report of the Seventeenth Decennial Census of the United States, Census Population: 1950, Volume II, Characteristics of the Population, Number of Inhabitants, General and Detailed Characteristics of the Population, Part 30, New Jersey.* Washington: United States Government Printing Office.

———. 1953. *United States Census Population:1950: Special Reports, Employment and Personal Characteristics, 1950 Population Census Report P-E No. 1A.* Pre print of Volume IV, Part I, Chapter A. Washington: United States Government Printing Office.

E. Musical Compositions and Recordings (print, tape, discography)

Ambrose, Stanley G. I. Clark, F. A., arranger. 1931. *Somewhere There Is A City.* Sheet music.

———. 1931. *I Have A Home.* Sheet music.

Davis, S. Edward. 1937–1962. Woodbury Choral Society annual concerts. Woodbury, NJ. Unpublished reel-to-reel audiotapes.

Foster, Allen Sr. *Bradley.* Hymn tune. 1985. In *Seventh-day Adventist Hymnal.* Washington, D.C.: Review and Herald Publishing Association. Hymn 298, title: *I lay my sins on Jesus.*

———. *Challenged.* Hymn tune. 1985. In *Seventh-day Adventist Hymnal.* Washington, D.C.: Review and Herald Publishing Association. Hymn 203, title: *This is the threefold truth.*

————. *Finally.* Hymn tune. 1985. In *Seventh-day Adventist Hymnal.* Washington, D.C.: Review and Herald Publishing Association. Hymn 417, title: *O solemn thought.*

————. *Jesus Walked this Lonesome Valley.* Arr. 1985. In *Seventh-day Adventist Hymnal.* Washington, D.C.: Review and Herald Publishing Association. Hymn 151.

Ingram Enterprise. 1970–1980. Choir concerts of various Camden, NJ churches. Unpublished reel-to-reel audiotapes.

————. 1978. *Ecumenical Choir: Recorded Live in Concert.* Camden, NJ. 331/3 LP phonorecord.

Ingram, N. Henry Sr. 1970–1991. *Words and Music.* Camden, NJ. WKDN radio broadcasts, priv. collection N. Henry Ingram, Jr. Audiotape.

Little, J. Ferman. Little, Mary E., lyrics, Moore, Mary E. Lacy, arranger. 1948. *Let the Drop From Heaven Fall On Me.* Washington, D.C.

————, 1990–1995. Unpublished collection of hymns. Digital tape.

Kershaw, Charles V. 1950–1970. *The Kershaw Hour.* Camden, NJ. WKDN radio broadcasts, priv. collection N. Henry Ingram, Jr. Audiotape.

King, Betty Jackson. 1973. *A Lullaby for You.* Chicago, IL: Jacksonian Press, Inc. Sheet music.

————. 1969. *The Nuptial Suite: for Organ.* Chicago, IL: Jacksonian Press, Inc. Sheet music.

————. *Saul of Tarsus: A Biblical Opera.* Chicago, IL: Jacksonian Press, Inc. Sheet music.

————. *My Servant Job: A Biblical Opera.* Chicago, IL: Jacksonian Press, Inc. Sheet music.

————. *Simon of Cyrene.* Chicago, IL: Jacksonian Press, Inc. Sheet music.

————. *Four Seasonal Sketches.* Chicago, IL: Jacksonian Press, Inc. Sheet music.

————. *Calvary (spiritual).* Arrangement. 1994. In *Watch and pray: spirituals and art songs by African-American women composers.* Videmus. Koch International Classics 372472H1. Compact disk.

————. *It's me, O Lord (spiritual).* Arrangement. 1994. In *Watch and pray: spirituals and art songs by African-American women composers.* Videmus. Koch International Classics 372472H1. Compact disk.

————. *Springtime.* 1994. In *Watch and pray: spirituals and art songs by African-American women composers.* Videmus. Koch International Classics 372472H1. Compact disk.

Secondary Sources

A. Books and Pamphlets

Butler, Rebecca Batts. 1980. *Profiles of outstanding Blacks in South Jersey during the 1950's, 1960's, 1970's.* Reynolds Publishers.

———. 1985. *Portraits of Black Role Models in the History of Southern New Jersey.* Wilmington, DE: Acme Craftsmen Publishers.

Gladolich, Richard M. 1986. *By Rail to the Boardwalk.* Glendale, CA: Trans-Anglo Books.

Hooper, Wayne and White, Edward E., ed. 1988. *Companion to the Seventh-day Adventist Hymnal.* Washington, D.C.: Review and Herald Publishing Association.

Jones, Robert. 1894. *Fifty Years in the Lombard Street Central Presbyterian Church.* Philadelphia, PA: Edward Stern & Co.

Kaighn Avenue Baptist Church. History Committee. n.d. *History of the Kaighn Avenue Baptist Church.* Camden, NJ. Pamphlet.

Mother Bethel African Methodist Episcopal Church. n.d. *Mother Bethel AME Church: The Mother Church of African Methodism.* Philadelphia, PA. Pamphlet.

The New Jersey Guild Associates. 1986. *The WPA Guide to 1930's New Jersey: compiled and written by the Federal Writers' Project of the Works Progress Administration for the State of New Jersey.* Reprint, original title *New Jersey, a guide to its present and past.* New Brunswick: Rutgers University Press.

Southern, Eileen. 1983. *The Music Of Black Americans: A History.* Second edition. New York: W.W. Norton & Company.

Wright, Giles R. 1988. *Afro-Americans in New Jersey: A Short History.* Trenton, N.J.: New Jersey Historical Commission.

B. Databases-Computer, Electronic, CD-Rom, Print

Alumni Records. Alumni Records Office, Temple University, Philadelphia, PA. Computer and print. Via telephone inquiry.

Computrace. 1995. Santa Ana, CA: CDB Infotek, Inc. Online. Accessed via Compuserve Jun 1995. Available by HTTP at http://www.cdb.com/

U.S. Department of Health and Human Services, Social Security Administration. 1995. "U.S. Social Security Death Index", *FamilySearch*. Salt Lake City, UT: Family History Department, The Church of Jesus Christ of Latter-Day Saints. CD-Rom. May 1996.

"New Jersey Death Index," *Nationwide Death Index*. 1996. CSRA, Inc. CD-Rom. Online. New Jersey State Library, Trenton, NJ. Jun 1996.

Student enrollment records. Office of the Registrar. Fisk University, Nashville, TN. Computer and print. Via telephone inquiry.

Index

Index

A

Allison, Theodora M. 30–34, 139
Ambrose, Stanley G. 13, 34–40, 145, 146
Anderson, Marian 9, 22, 50, 141

B

Berlin Junior Harmony Four 37
Blair, Ellen Dixon-Hodge 40–42, 136
Borden Bellringers 48
Brown, Emily Lucken 18, 21, 42–49, 126, 136
Burleigh, Harry T. 51, 57
Butler, Rebecca Batts Dr. 25

C

Camden County Historical Society xiv
Campbell Soup Male Glee Club 113–116

Churches, New Jersey
 Allen AME Church, Williamstown 42
 Antioch Christian Community Church, Chesilhurst 16
 Asbury Methodist Church, Pennsauken 70, 115, 127
 Baptist Temple Church, Camden 45, 80, 96, 129
 Bethany Baptist Church, Burlington 148
 Bethany Baptist Church, Somerdale 100
 Bethel AME Church, Camden 45, 102, 115
 Bethel AME Church, Moorestown 34, 35, 115
 Bethel AME Church, Paulsboro 42
 Bethel AME Church, Woodbury 56
 Bethel Methodist Church, Camden 115
 Bethlehem Baptist Church, Woodbury 74, 83
 Beulah Baptist Church, Camden 79
 Broadway United Methodist Church, Camden 20, 42, 130, 150
 Calvary Baptist Church, West Atco 16, 64, 68

Part III

F

Fernandez (Fernanders), Juanita Alvera 41, 47, 68–71, 136
Foster, Allen William Sr. 71–74
Fraction, Edward Arthur Jr. 18, 74–78

G

Givens, Audrey Canois 42, 78–81, 136

H

Hackley, Azalia 140
Hamilton, Jesse I. Jr. 73, 81–85, 94, 136, 150
Hamilton, Jesse I. Sr. 85–90, 130
Harris, Lois Custis 84, 91–94, 137, 141, 150
Hayes, Roland 22, 111, 141
Holmes, Roberta Jones 18, 21, 95–97, 129, 143
Hunton Branch Symphony Orchestra, YMCA Camden 47, 71, 136
Hunton Branch WPA Band, YMCA Camden 136

I

Ingram Enterprise 99
Ingram, N. Henry Sr. 48, 97–101

J

James, Lottie Price 21, 100–103
Johnson, Hall 51, 53, 112, 143
Johnson, W. Russell 141
Judimar School of Dance, Philadelphia 64

K

Kershaw Hour 18, 47, 98, 146
Kershaw Royal Singers 48, 99, 146
King, Betty Jackson 22, 103–106

L

Little, J. Ferman 106-110

M